GHOST HUNTING IN THE
BLACK COUNTRY
AND BEYOND

Ghost Hunting in the
Black Country
and Beyond

ANDREW HOMER

Tin Typewriter

Tin Typewriter Publishing

Copyright © 2022 Andrew Homer

First published 2022
Tin Typewriter Publishing
Plymouth
www.tintypewriter.co.uk

ISBN: 978-1-911309-19-2

CONTENTS

ACKNOWLEDGEMENTS

I am very grateful to anyone who has helped in any way even if it was only jogging my memory on occasions! In particular though, I must thank Steve Potter and Mark Hunt for permission to use their photographs. Also, Michael Lewis for permission to use extracts from his book *Conclusions of a Parapsychologist* in connection with our investigations at Belgrave in Leicester. I am also grateful to Steve Ford for his excellent DVD *Gunpowder Ghost - the legend of the Wombourne Phantom*. Also, the very talented Joe Healy for kindly providing the spooky music for the video clips.

Thanks also to Lizzie Whitehouse for details of the figure seen on the Black Country Living Museum boat dock together with Chris Cooper for stories collected by Brian Perry. I am also particularly grateful to friends and fellow paranormal investigator's George Gregg, Dennis Bache, Frank Smith and Steve Willis who will all be found in the text. Thanks also to my daughter, Sophie Homer, for coming up with the idea of using QR codes and to Onshell Relf for advice on producing the video clips.

The investigations recounted in this book and many others over the years were conducted in conjunction with a number of exceptional paranormal research groups. Many members of these groups remain lifelong friends. In alphabetical order:

- Association for the Scientific Study of Anomalous Phenomena (ASSAP)
- Coventry Paranormal Investigators (CPI)
- Parasearch
- Stourbridge Independent Paranormal Society (SIPS)
- The Ghost Club
- West Midlands Ghost Club

The vast majority of images are from Andrew Homer's own personal collection and every effort has been made to ascertain copyright ownership and credit accordingly. Any due acknowledgement which has been inadvertently omitted or any unintentional infringement of copyright will be corrected in future copies of this work.

INTRODUCTION

The idea to write *Ghost hunting in the Black Country and Beyond* came about mainly due to feedback from the successful *Black Country Ghosts and Hauntings* by the same author. Readers were commenting that it would be interesting to find out more about the various investigations into paranormal activity mentioned in the book. This book then is about what really happened when experienced paranormal investigators were given access to some amazing properties. Mainly due to the immense popularity of television shows such as *Most haunted*, ghost hunting has changed almost beyond recognition in a relatively short space of time. Whereas we were mostly invited in to investigate phenomena as it was occurring, locations are now more likely to be booked by paranormal event companies. Nowadays, it is possible for anyone to pay for an organised ghost hunt in buildings which previously would only have been open to established research groups.

This is not necessarily a bad thing, as there is clearly a great deal of interest and many of the locations in this book now host organised 'ghost hunting' events. However, in the author's experience, paranormal activity is far from reliable and established ghost stories often bear little or no resemblance to what is actually happening when a site is active. We were fortunate during our investigations that we were generally called in because the locations were actively experiencing periods of paranormal activity.

This book chronicles well over 25 years of investigating anomalous phenomena in a variety of locations in conjunction with various paranormal research groups. Many were investigated more than once and some on multiple occasions over a long period of time. For brevity, only the relatively few occasions that something potentially paranormal was witnessed or recorded have been included. In the same vein, cases where we were able to determine what the anomaly actually was have also been included. The classic example here being the remarkable Wem 'Girl in the Flames' photograph taken whilst Wem Town Hall was burning down. There were many more allegedly haunted locations with credible reports but sadly yielded no results of any significance when we investigated, and so these have been omitted.

This would have been a very boring book indeed if it included all the long, dark, often cold nights spent in allegedly haunted locations with only the occasional break for coffee to relieve the monotony!

Because active cases were generally being referred to us, in one or two instances we were asked not to divulge the locations and the people involved. In these cases, pseudonyms are used together with fictitious place names. All other details of the cases are correct and recorded at the time.

In addition to Wem Town Hall there are some very well-known haunted locations within these pages. In the Black Country there is Dudley Castle, West Bromwich Manor House, and the Black Country Living Museum whilst further afield we have the Ancient Ram Inn, Belgrave Hall and Woodchester Mansion to name but a few of the fascinating cases recorded here.

Look out for the video symbol 🎥 which denotes actual location footage available on YouTube. This footage can be accessed simply by scanning the QR codes with a suitable mobile phone application. Alternatively type in the links at the end of the book to access the YouTube video clips.

This book then records the highlights of those occasions when something 'other worldly' really did manifest itself whilst *Ghost Hunting in the Black Country and Beyond.*

ENCOUNTER WITH A GHOST NR BRIERLEY HILL

Ancient Ram Inn

The Ancient Ram Inn at Wotton-under-Edge in Gloucestershire regularly makes any top ten of most haunted places in Britain. It is everything you would expect a haunted house to be, with darkened wooden beams, low ceilings, narrow twisted stairs, and dimly lit rooms. All this and more creates an oppressive atmosphere where even the most sceptical might think twice about the possibility of ghosts. And there are plenty here to choose from if all the stories are to be believed.

Ancient Ram Inn

Precisely dating the Grade II listed Ancient Ram is difficult but parts of it could well go back to the 12ᵗʰ century. The Historic England listing refers to an ecclesiastical connection with the local church and it may have initially housed masons and other workers building St Mary the Virgin. Later it is said to have housed the local clergy which might have led to the naming of the Bishop's Room, a focus for much of the hauntings. There is no shortage of legends regarding its early origins including being built on a Pagan burial ground, on converging ley lines and the diversion of streams said to generate negative energy. The building later became an inn although ceased to be licensed premises in the 1960s when it was purchased by the late John

Humphries, whose intention was to preserve the ancient building. John was responsible for furnishing the rooms with period furniture, antiques, artefacts, and quirky, not to say gruesome, items which all add to the ghostly atmosphere. John was always pleased to see us and enjoyed nothing more than telling us the latest stories about his house full of ghosts, both friendly and decidedly otherwise.

The Bishop's Room

As befits its reputation, there are a plethora of ghosts associated with the Ancient Ram. One of these is said to be a witch who took refuge in one of rooms before being captured. She was burned at the stake, but her spirit still haunts what is now called 'The Witch's Room'. It has to be noted though that it was much more common for convicted witches to be hung rather than burned at the stake in this country. Other apparitions seen in the building include a former innkeeper but even more disturbing is the young girl seen hanging from one of the upstairs rooms. The Bishop's Room is said to be the most haunted of all with monks and nuns together with a soldier described as a cavalier who is seen standing in the corner before disappearing through the wall. Add in phantom highwaymen and demonic entities that try to pull people out of bed and it is easy to see why John's idea of a historic bed and breakfast never really took off, especially when guests were packing up and leaving in the early hours of the morning!

Poltergeist activity comes as almost an afterthought here, with reports of doors banging, knocking on the windows and mysterious pools of water appearing. John believed he had discovered evidence of Satanic rituals and black magic in the building which might explain the increase in paranormal activity when he bought a portrait of Methodist leader John Wesley to hang on the stairs. Anomalous lights and white mists are also seen in various parts of the building. There is enough paranormal activity reported in the Ancient Ram to fill a book on its own. No wonder then it is such a desired destination for paranormal groups and individuals alike.

The Ancient Ram, at least when we were there, was often freezing cold especially in the winter. On one particularly cold night it actually felt warmer outside! Rechargeable batteries would often not function for as long as expected especially when operating higher current equipment such as the low light video recorders. This is sometimes reported as paranormal, especially when the batteries seem to recover once removed from the haunted location. In the author's experience it is more the case that certain types of rechargeable batteries simply do not function well in the cold but will recover well once returned to a warmer environment.

The author often joined Mark and Julie Hunt who conducted many investigations at the Ancient Ram and who knew John quite well.

On one such investigation Julie was keen to get some pictures of the stairs after we had finished a vigil session in the Bishop's Room. The photographs, including the one pictured were all taken on Julie's Canon TLB Single Lens Reflex (SLR) camera, and she was using fairly fast 400 ASA film This was quite a large 35 mm film camera. Being SLR, the image seen in the viewfinder is through the lens and a mirror moves out of the way when the picture is taken. Therefore, what is seen in the viewfinder is what appears on the film. Had there been anything obscuring the lens to the extent of the misty image, it would have been clearly seen. I can certainly confirm that there was nothing visible on the stairs at the time. The image appeared on only one frame of the roll of film when it was developed.

Picture taken by Julie Hunt (Courtesy of Mark Hunt)

Small compact film cameras with a separate viewfinder were prone to things such as the camera strap obscuring the lens and being illuminated by the small inbuilt flash, but these problems simply did not apply to SLR cameras such as the one used by Julie. It is also interesting to note that such misty shapes are a feature of the activity at the Ancient Ram.

Amongst the plethora of ghostly sightings and paranormal activity are, in the words of the late John Humphries, "strange glowing lights". It is rare for investigators to experience reported phenomena first hand for themselves, but the Ancient Ram proved to be one of those rare exceptions for paranormal investigator Steve Willis and the author. We had previously experienced random, unexplained flashes of light in a downstairs room called the Gentleman's Kitchen, but then one night:

It was about 10.15 pm at the start of the investigation, and we were busying ourselves transporting video equipment from the car into the inn. One of the areas we were keen to investigate was the Bishop's Room upstairs, where reputedly few ever stay the whole night. Access to this room was through an area quaintly named the Gentleman's

Kitchen from the days when the Ancient Ram was still functioning as an inn.

Carrying a large and quite heavy box of infrared video equipment through this darkened room on the way upstairs we were both surprised to see a round glowing ball, yellow in colour and about the size of a large light bulb, moving silently just below the ceiling. It travelled slowly for a couple of metres across the room and then simply disappeared. We both had a clear view of the glowing ball of light so we can at least conclude that it was an objective phenomenon that we experienced that night.

Of course, having state of the art low light video recording equipment is of little use if it is still in the box when something interesting actually happens!

Beacon Hotel, Sedgley

Research for the *Beer and Spirits* book which was published in 2010, took me to the Beacon Hotel in Sedgley where I was living at the time. The Beacon is a rare surviving example of a mid-Victorian public house complete with its own tower brewery which is still in use brewing under the name of Sarah Hughes. The pub and brewery were bought at Auction by Sarah in 1921 and is still owned by the Hughes family who take great pains to preserve the Beacon's traditional character.

The Beacon Hotel and Sarah Hughes Brewery

A realistic portrait of Sarah Hughes resides in the building and according to one of the previous managers, so does the ghost of Sarah herself. He claimed to have seen her walking through a wall in the smoke room in the exact spot where there had once been a door.

Before internal alarms and CCTV were fitted, it was common practice for duty managers to sleep over in the downstairs sitting room. One of the former managers, Andy, related the following incident:

In the summer of 1994 when I was managing the Beacon the owner used to be away every few weeks. On these occasions he liked one of the staff to stop on the premises overnight for security and quite often it was me. I usually slept in the sitting room. In that room is a painting of Sarah Hughes in which the eyes seem to follow you round the room. I suppose you never sleep properly when you are on protection duty, and something woke me. My alarm clock showed 3.00 am.

Opening my eyes, I took a quick glance around the room. In the comer by the door onto the passage stood a figure. After a couple of seconds, I realised that they had not broken into the pub, or the outside alarms would be shrieking. I don't know how long I looked at the figure. It was a man in his fifties wearing wellington boots, dark trousers and a grey or white shirt with an old fashioned, round, grandad style collar and a waistcoat. I have always thought that ghosts were transparent, but he looked quite solid. Suddenly grasping what I was seeing, my heart raced, and I shut my eyes tight. When I looked again a few seconds later the figure had vanished.

I told my dad about the night visitor and described what he was wearing, and he said it sounded like the father of the present owner, who liked to go about in old fashioned clothes.

More frequently though it is low level poltergeist type activity that is experienced in the pub. Loud footsteps are heard when there is nobody there and small objects disappear and then reappear in odd circumstances. Shortly before my visit to get the stories for the book, just such an incident had taken place.

There is a large key which locks the inner doors to the pub and is always kept in a particular place behind the bar. On opening up one morning this key was nowhere to be found and the spare had to be brought in. Towards afternoon closing the duty manager and a small group of customers were the only people in the pub. They were all in the large smoke room at the rear. All of a sudden, from behind the bar came a loud clatter of something metallic falling or being thrown to the ground. The missing key was now in the middle of the floor behind the bar! No explanation could be found as there was nobody behind or around the bar at the time and the key was clearly heard by all to be dropped or thrown.

Staff and customers alike claim to have heard bumps and bangs from upstairs and the sound of someone standing on a loose floorboard, although these days the rooms are only used only for storage. In between talking to barman, Adrian, about stories for the *Beer and Spirits* book the author heard these noises without realising what they were. "At first, I took no notice of the sounds, though they were quite loud. It sounded as though someone was walking around and moving heavy furniture about upstairs". Later the same evening a casual remark to Adrian about the noises revealed the story and confirmed that there had definitely been nobody upstairs all evening.

The Black Country Living Museum

The Black Country Living Museum started life on wasteland near Dudley in the 1970s and first opened for a preview season in 1978. Since then, the majority of buildings on the site have been moved from their original locations. Buildings are taken down brick by brick, piece by piece, with everything carefully coded so they can be reassembled on the museum site. Thus, most of the buildings are original but no longer in their original location. Logically, it would be reasonable to expect such buildings to be free of any paranormal activity. This is not the case, however, as both staff (including the author) and visitors have reported experiences which certainly come under the heading of ghosts and hauntings. Often the best way to investigate a site is simply to be there regularly as the author found when he was a member of staff. Are these experiences somehow stored in the buildings themselves?

The term Stone Tape Theory suggests that events, particularly traumatic ones, can somehow be stored in the very fabric of the surroundings in which they took place, and subsequently be replayed under certain circumstances. Over the years, Stone Tape Theory has very largely been discredited by science on the basis that there is no known mechanism whereby such recordings could be stored in, for example, the brickwork of buildings. Stone Tape Theory is sometimes wrongly attributed to 'The Stone Tape', a BBC drama first aired in 1972. The name may well be traced back to this drama but the writer, Nigel Kneale, was most certainly not responsible for proposing the notion that buildings could somehow store earlier events.

In fact, no one person can be reliably credited with this idea. Certainly, the theory is often attributed to Thomas Charles Lethbridge, an archaeologist and later parapsychologist. In his 1961 book, *Ghost and Ghoul*, Lethbridge makes the connection between memories and inanimate objects. Lethbridge himself cited work done by Oxford Professor and former President of the Society for Psychical Research, H. H. Price. It was Price who came up with the concept of 'place memories'. Detached memories becoming somehow attached to the environment and played back as hallucinations under the right circumstances. In fact, such ideas can be traced right back to the early days of the Society for Psychical Research (SPR) which was formed in 1882.

Despite the lack of any evidence for Stone Tape Theory or place memories, there are a number of well documented sightings from buildings at the Black Country Living Museum and other similar museums of buildings such as Avoncroft Museum of Historic Buildings in Bromsgrove – at least according to staff there interviewed by the author.

Toll House moved from Woodsetton

One of the first domestic buildings to be encountered on a visit to the Black Country Living Museum site is the former Toll House originally from Woodsetton and dating back to 1845. Once the turnpike road it served had been taken over by the local council in the 1870s, there was no more need for toll house keepers and the little cottage was just rented out.

On one occasion some years back, a lady asked if she could look in what is called Lillian's bedroom as the door was closed. She opened the door and immediately closed it. When asked why she hadn't stepped inside the lady said she didn't want to disturb the girl sleeping on the bed. The room was empty.

Working in the building, the author was often asked if it was haunted. Very often visitors would ask if one particular room was haunted. It was always the bedroom to the right on entering through the front door. On one occasion two visitors asking the same question got a surprise:

It was a cold winter afternoon at the museum and being later on in the day was getting fairly quiet. A couple came in and started asking about ghosts as someone had told them about the bedroom. I had just started to relate the story of the girl on the bed, when we all heard three very distinct knocks on wood coming from the bedroom. There was nobody else inside the building or outside as we could see through the windows. The couple were delighted that they had heard something! About ten minutes later, the same thing happened again. Three distinct knocks coming from inside the bedroom. By this time, the couple had gone and there was nobody in sight. I went to look and there was nothing there. When it happened the third time, I climbed over the barrier and stood in the bedroom for some minutes hoping it would reoccur. Of course, it didn't. On speaking to an older colleague about it, he told me that after it had ceased to be a Toll House a family with a very wilful daughter rented it. The bedroom has a large, built-in wall cupboard with wooden doors. Apparently, they would lock her in this cupboard as punishment. If it happened again, I was going to look inside the cupboard but it never did.

St James's School moved from Dudley

Further down the same road is St James's School. Over the years there have been reports of a wounded American soldier seen in the first classroom. This has been in broad daylight but as soon as the soldier is noticed he disappears. The connection with American soldiers may seem odd, but in World War Two Americans were stationed in Dudley before the D-Day landings and the school was taken over for their use.

The museum often runs extremely popular night-time events. If the school has been used it has to be locked up afterwards. The light switches are in the second classroom, so the building has to be put into darkness before whoever does it has to walk back through the two classrooms by torchlight to get to the main door. Staff have often had the intense feeling of someone watching them as they do this. On many occasions, the person locking up on their own has left the building a good deal quicker than they went in.

The Workers' Institute moved from Cradley Heath

At the other end of the 1930's street to the school is the impressive Worker's Institute. This is the largest building open to visitors and as well as telling the story of the women chainmakers' strike of 1910 and their charismatic leader, Mary Macarthur, it also houses the main onsite café. When the author first started working at the museum the café would close an hour before the building was fully locked up for the night. Often, there would be no visitors during this last hour and so the costumed character assigned to the building would be left to sweep up and lock the front door. It was quite common in this quiet period to hear bumps, bangs and occasionally sounds like footsteps echoing through the empty building. Most of these could be put down to the building settling except on one occasion:

> I had begun sweeping and closing down upstairs in the Committee Room. Having closed the doors, the next job was to sweep Mary's Office. Mary Macarthur never had an office here, but it was set up in the 1930s as a memorial to Mary. The doors don't lock but the period door furniture means that they do shut securely. Next job was to sweep down the wooden staircase. As I was doing so, I heard the sound of someone coming in through the front door. Nothing unusual in that as we did get occasional late visitors. However, I suddenly felt something brush past me quickly on the stairs although I didn't see anything. This was followed almost immediately by the door to Mary's office just above me not just opening but slamming hard into the cupboard next to it as though someone in a great temper had burst in. Of course, when I went to look there was nobody there. This was not the end to it though. Back in the downstairs office there was still a few minutes before locking up time. As I sat behind the desk something started chiming. My mobile phone was on silent, and I realised it was the period mantlepiece clock. Now this clock would keep quite good time if wound every morning with its separate key, but although it had a chime it was broken. If wound, the chime would just ring out until the spring had unwound. This is what the clock was doing but I certainly hadn't wound the chime. All this in the space of no more than five minutes. Although I was to spend a great deal more time in the Worker's Institute these events never repeated themselves.

Another odd event that occurred in the Worker's Institute was witnessed by the author, a visitor, and another member of staff.

> It was lunch time and I had arranged to meet with a colleague, Dave, in the Worker's Institute Café. I was stood in the queue very close to the checkout. In front of me were some delicious looking cakes on glass cake stands covered by large glass domes. Without anyone

touching it, the dome in front of me lifted off the stand as though someone had picked it up and went towards the lady standing next to me. She tried to catch it, but it slipped through her fingers and smashed to the floor. Now, the obvious explanation would be that the glass dome had simply slipped off the base. However, the cake underneath, a large Victoria sponge, had not moved on the stand and suffered no damage from the glass dome. The dome would need to have been lifted up over the cake for this to happen. I hadn't realised that my friend Dave had also seen the whole incident and was equally baffled.

Below the 1930's street is the canalside village with its range of shops, chapel, and pub. Next to the chapel is Emile Doo's Chemist Shop. It was here, early one morning that a member of staff was making her way to work. As she walked past the shop, she couldn't help but notice three old ladies in extremely authentic Victorian costume chatting away inside. Naturally assuming they were costumed staff she looked away but on looking back they had vanished. A tall, slim lady in a black dress has also been seen by staff standing on the path between the Chemist Shop and Providence Chapel. Although she appears to be a real person, once the witness looks away and back again, she also is gone.

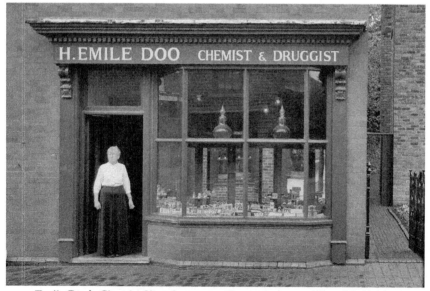

Emile Doo's Chemist Shop frontage and contents moved from Netherton

Opposite the Chemist is the Hardware Shop. This building had a varied past and was moved from Piper's Row in Wolverhampton, an area which once had a rather unsavoury reputation. When first starting to work in there the author was advised to listen out for the footsteps coming from upstairs. As the costume department was situated upstairs it seemed most unlikely that there was anything unusual in hearing footsteps from up there.

The first time I heard the footsteps it was late one Sunday. There were no visitors in the shop at the time and the footsteps went diagonally across the floor above, exactly as my colleague had described. As the shop was empty, I was immediately able to go and check if anyone was upstairs as unlikely this would be on a Sunday. Apart from the shop front, there is only one other entrance and that was locked. Similarly, the rooms upstairs were also locked meaning there couldn't possibly be anyone up there. I heard the footsteps on a few occasions after that but was never able to discover who or what it was.

The Hardware Shop building moved from Wolverhampton

The Bottle and Glass Inn moved from Brockmoor

The Bottle and Glass Inn started life in Brockmoor, Brierley Hill before being moved to the museum. It has long been subject to paranormal activity. This seems to be centred on the back room where the sound of someone moving around is often heard when the room is empty. Much of the activity is childish such as tapping people on the back. Ladies in costume sometimes report having their long dresses pulled even though there is nobody there. If indeed it is a child, then it may be ten-year-old Isaac Male. He worked for canal boatman James Haines, by all accounts a hard taskmaster.

One foggy night, Haines and two of his men were leading their horse back to its stable after securing the narrowboat it had been pulling. Young Isaac had been allowed to ride on his back, but the horse lost his footing on the towpath and slipped into the canal with the poor boy desperately clinging on for dear life. The horse fell badly, trapping Isaac beneath him. Horses were valuable but little boys less so. Haines and his men took nearly twenty minutes to get the horse out of the canal without injury. By the time they gave any attention to Isaac it was too late, he had already drowned. His lifeless body was carried to the nearest pub and laid on a table in the back room of the Bottle and Glass. It was common practice to hold inquests in public houses as late as 1907 even after the practice was effectively discontinued by the Licensing Act 1902. It was so in this case, and the inquest was also held in the Bottle and Glass where little Isaac had been carried. The verdict was accidental death although Haines and his men were severely criticised for their actions, or lack of, that night. Reason enough perhaps for young Isaac Male to still be making his presence felt in the Bottle and Glass Inn.

Whilst recording a shortened version of the Isaac Male story for a Halloween publicity video in the Bottle and Glass we experienced some unaccounted-for noise in the back room. The 'Spooky Blooper' can be heard at the very end of the clip together with the author's reaction! 🎥 1   There were only three of us in the pub at the time and all in the back room. Could it be that little Isaac Male was trying to make his presence felt?

From the Bottle and Glass, Station Road leads down to the Museum's own canal boat dock. This is itself subject to sightings of a mysterious figure. Historic characters working on the canal arm sometimes see a man in working clothes climbing down into one of the narrowboats. He has been reported as wearing a white shirt with braces and black trousers.

On one occasion, he was clearly observed from the rear and spoken to whilst entering Kildare, an un-powered butty boat. He was seen to apparently open the doors and disappear into the narrowboat. On immediately checking, not only was there nobody in the boat but the doors he went through were securely locked.

If visiting the Black Country Museum, which is highly recommended, do not necessarily assume that all of the costumed characters you see are present day members of staff or volunteers!

🎥 1

Stourbridge Bonded Warehouse

The Bonded Warehouse with its semi-circular façade is a distinctive three-storey building situated at the end of the Stourbridge Town Canal Arm. It was built during the heyday of the canal system and allowed large amounts of goods to be transported around the country economically.

Stourbridge Town Canal Arm

The oldest parts of the building date back to 1799 with walls up to 13 inches thick. It was used to securely store transported goods awaiting collection including taxable items such as tobacco, spirits, and tea. These would be held until the appropriate excise duties had been paid. The coming of the railways eventually led to the decline of the canal network for transporting goods and the Bonded Warehouse was near derelict by the 1960s. It was thanks to the efforts of the Stourbridge Navigation Trust voluntary group the now Grade II listed building has been preserved as a community resource and hosts a wide range of large and small-scale events throughout the year.

There have been many reports of paranormal activity at the warehouse by both staff and visitors alike. Doors are prone to opening and closing on their own and objects get inexplicably moved around. In addition, the ghost of an old man has been seen in and around the building. He has been described by witnesses as having the appearance of an old boatman perhaps from the days when the Stourbridge Town Canal Arm was bustling with working narrowboats. The ghost of a young girl has also been seen, albeit fleetingly, skipping and playing on the top floor of the warehouse.

The Bonded Warehouse

Our first investigation at the Bonded Warehouse yielded some interesting results. All of the activity was situated on the upper floor of the building. This is a very large open space beneath heavy wooden roof trusses which span the width of the building. A proximity detector had been placed near the centre of the room well away from the small team situated up there. For a period of time, the detector was going off as it would if anyone approached. Although nothing was seen at this point, it seemed very much like something was moving quickly in and out of the field of detection. It was whilst this was going on that one of our team briefly saw the old boatman sitting on one of the roof trusses with his feet on the beam. As unlikely as this might seem, it is highly probable that the sturdy beams were once boarded across to provide extra storage space and he might have been sitting on an earlier level.

Although only glimpsed very briefly, the description tallied with other sightings of the old boatman.

The roof trusses on the top floor

A later investigation provided what may be tangible evidence of the little girl's presence on the top floor. We were a very small group with free access to the whole building for an overnight investigation. We split into two small groups and took it in turns to spend 45-minute vigil sessions upstairs and downstairs respectively.

I was wearing a night vision headcam unit which was excellent for continuously recording sound and vision. Just after midnight our group was due upstairs. I stayed behind briefly in the base room because I needed to change batteries and SD card in the headcam and it was much easier to do this with the lights on. Having changed everything, I made my way up the stairs. Everything was in darkness, so I was using a torch with a red filter to preserve night vision whilst moving around. On reaching the top floor I realised that the rest of the group were elsewhere. They actually turned out to be sitting in a side room.

At this point I was not aware that there was a trigger object in the middle of the upper floor. This consisted of a chair with a child's ball placed on it. The idea being that it might prove tempting to the little girl especially as things are known to be moved around in there. As I stood in the darkness at the edge of the room to switch my headcam back on I heard the sound of something bouncing loudly on the floor five or six times. When the rest of the group appeared and explained it was a trigger object, we found the ball some distance away from the chair. It turned out that the trigger object had been on the chair for over an hour previously without moving. We reset the ball of course but it did not bounce off again for the rest of the night.

I did not expect the incident to have been recorded as I was in the process of turning on the headcam when it happened. In the event though the recording starts just in time to record the whole thing and also to show that there was nobody anywhere near the trigger object when it happened. 🎥 1

Did the little girl make her presence felt in the upstairs room of the Bonded Warehouse that night? I certainly like to think so.

🎥 1

Bridgnorth Road Ghost

Phantom hitchhiker reports are regarded by many researchers to be more folklore or urban myth than actual events. Often, they are reported at least second or third hand in the form of 'friend of a friend' stories. Blue Bell Hill in Kent is well known for its phantom hitchhiker stories but not so the Black Country and surrounding areas. In fact, the author is aware of only this one but was able to get the story direct from the witness for whom the experience was all too real. This account is taken directly from the author's interview with Stuart, an experienced coach driver. The interview came about because Stewart was keen to know if anyone could shed light on his strange experience, and everyone he had mentioned it to thus far had either treated it as a joke or knew nothing about road ghosts. He had no previous knowledge of phantom hitchhikers himself and was at least reassured that his experience was by no means unique.

The crossroads at Tinkers Castle

Phantom hitchhiker encounters often share common themes and Stuart's experience one dark Sunday night in October 2000 was no exception. Setting out from the coach station in Lower Gornal, Stuart picked up his passengers from around the Dudley area ready to take them for a booked meal and night out in Bridgnorth, Shropshire. The route was straightforward and took him along the B4176 known locally as the 'Rabbit Run' and then on to the A454 Bridgnorth Road. Stewart recalled seeing nothing untoward on the outward journey with very little traffic. Having dropped his passengers in Bridgnorth he decided to drive back to the coach station in Gornal for a coffee in the office rather than park up and wait. Following the same return route Stuart estimated it was about 8.30 pm when he was passing The Wheel at Worfield public house. Through the darkness Stuart could just make out the silhouette of a person illuminated in his headlights. Slowing the coach down as he drew closer, he could see it was a man carrying a petrol can. It was obvious the man had broken down somewhere and Stuart decided to stop and offer him a lift. The man climbed aboard and sat down in the courier seat. Even though the main coach lights were off Stuart noted the man's slightly strange appearance. In Stuart's own words:

He was dressed as though he had come straight from a 1960's or 1970's revival night which I thought was rather odd. He had a wide lapel shirt, bell bottomed trousers and an ear length George Best style of haircut. Just the sort of thing you would expect for a 60's or 70's disco night'. His passenger explained that he had been on his way home to Telford along the 'Rabbit Run' and had run out of petrol. The stranger was very grateful for the lift as he said he had a long walk back to his car.

We got to the island where you can go straight on for Wolverhampton, turn off left for Telford or turn right for Wombourne. There is a big pub [The Royal Oak] there on the corner. I asked him which way he was going as I was only really killing time and I said I'd drop him off at his car. He did say that the car was off towards Wombourne parked on the verge. I'd got to go that way anyway, so we proceeded up towards Tinkers Castle and sure enough, there on the right-hand side of the road, on the grass verge was a rather nice-looking Triumph TR7 sports car. My passenger said it was a TR8 and that it was pretty rare. I thought it was a TR7 but he was adamant it was a TR8. He also said that the car was a one off and was his absolute pride and joy.

The very rare Triumph TR8 Coupe had a V8 engine

This was right on the crossroads at Tinkers Castle. So, I pulled up more or less alongside the car, perhaps a little bit in front. He thanked me for giving him a lift and said it would have taken him ages to walk back there. He got off the coach, thanked me again, walked across the windscreen in front of me, waved and disappeared out of sight. Whilst pulling off I then glanced in the offside mirror and he'd gone, completely disappeared. I first thought it might have been a blind spot. With any heavy goods or large vehicle there is a blind spot, so I stopped and stuck my head right out of the window bearing in mind I'd only travelled a matter of a couple of yards. The road was straight so there wasn't a curve to obscure my view and he had definitely gone. I couldn't believe it. I looked right out of the window and there was nobody there on that crossroads. It was totally deserted. Not only that, but the sports car had completely and silently vanished too.

In the space of about 10 to 15 seconds he had got to get off the coach, walk around the front, cross the road, open his fuel cap, pour the petrol in, fasten it back, get in his car, turn the engine over to pump the petrol through and then drive off. All of this in about 10 to 15 seconds and with no sound of an engine starting. Well, I can tell you, the hairs on the back of my neck stood on end, I just couldn't believe it. I tried to get away as fast as I could, I was crashing the gears. I just couldn't get away from the area quick enough.

One of the main features of phantom hitchhiker experiences is that it all seems very real until, as in this case, the hitchhiker suddenly disappears. From Stuart's point of view this was real, and he even remembered getting a whiff of petrol from the can the man was carrying. Their conversation had been normal even though the stranger's clothes and hairstyle had been outdated. Stuart was also adamant that if the Triumph had been parked on the road by Tinker's Castle when he had passed by less than an hour previously, he would definitely have remembered it.

The only petrol station in the area is at Worfield which meant a walk of nearly five miles through the countryside back to the car. Stuart had been so bemused that he contacted the garage just to confirm that someone else had at least seen the strange character and sold him petrol. The manager told Stuart that the petrol station did not open on Sunday evenings, and had not done so for decades.

Castle Lodge Ludlow

Ludlow is a fascinating place with its historic buildings and medieval castle. Many claim to be haunted and none more so than the prominent Grade II listed Tudor house known as the Castle Lodge. Parts of the ground floor dates back to the 14th century whilst the overhanging timberwork is a striking 16th century addition. It is allegedly haunted by the young Catherine of Aragon who is said to have stayed there. She was certainly in Ludlow with Prince Arthur, elder brother to Henry, later Henry VIII. After their marriage in 1501, the young couple moved into comfortable royal apartments within Ludlow Castle. The marriage was short lived as Arthur died of a disease known as 'sweating sickness' Catherine was ill too but survived. If she stayed at the Castle Lodge at all it would most likely have been for a short time after Arthur's death although there is no evidence for this.

Figure 1 The imposing Castle Lodge Ludlow

The most well-known sighting attributed to Catherine took place on the upper floor of Castle Lodge. This later addition to the building was added by Robert Berry, an official of the Council of the Marches, many years after the widowed Catherine had left Ludlow. But this does not mean that a Tudor ghost was not seen, it simply could not have been Catherine of Aragon.

The upper floor where Gwen Pearson saw her Tudor ghost

In fact, the apparition of a young lady in what appears to be Tudor dress has been glimpsed by visitors to Castle Lodge. Looking like a costumed guide, witnesses only realise they have actually seen a ghost when she suddenly n disappears through a wall.

One of the most detailed sightings of this apparition was made by the late wife of the owner at the time, Bill Pearson. Former Prima Ballerina, Gwen Pearson, was able to provide an incredibly detailed description of the young lady. Initially, she had thought someone had got locked in after closing up for the day. It was only when the solid looking figure disappeared through the wall that Gwen realised she was the ghost. Before Bill sadly passed away the author was able to interview him and get the full details of Gwen's remarkable sighting:

The figure was about 5ft tall. She was wearing a golden collar but a man's cloak according to fashion books of the time. It was a cloak for going out in. Underneath she was well dressed. She had this golden, woollen, high quality dress. Her hair was gathered in a snood or net. She had something around her neck, a single stone that sparkled, probably a single diamond. The strange thing was she was wearing red gauntlets and hanging from the gauntlets there was a chord with a big red bobble on the end of each one. She seemed very happy and not pale as in the pictures but quite ruddy faced. She seemed very happy, skipping, and running along the corridor before disappearing through the wall.

Our group was very fortunate to be invited by Bill to do a full day's investigation at Castle Lodge. During the day, a reporter from BBC Radio Shropshire arrived to do an interview about our activities. I agreed to do this having explained to the presenter that we were a serious scientific group and certainly not a bunch of 'Ghostbusters'. The reporter agreed to treat the interview seriously and indeed the interview seemed to go well. It was due to go out the same evening and as we had no radio, phoned another member to record it for us. Ignoring everything I had said, the studio presenter introduced the piece as follows:

"A team of Ghostbusters has been called in to investigate ghostly goings on at Ludlow Castle. The group from Parasearch set up camp today at the Castle Lodge after a number of sightings of ghosts in the historic buildings."

"Hello, I'm Andrew from Parasearch", accompanied by the theme from the *Ghostbusters* movie.

What was transmitted was so amusing that the recording has since been used in numerous presentations!

It was on the upper floor that Gwen saw her apparition and visitors too report all sorts of strange experiences particularly around the oddly shaped room at the end of the landing by the stairs.

The oddly shaped room at the end of the top floor corridor

People have reported feelings of not being alone, cold spots, and the sound of loud footsteps even when nobody else is up there. During our investigation there the author had the following experience:

Around lunchtime people went off to get something to eat but I opted to take advantage of the quiet building and stayed behind. I was sitting at the very top of the stairs on the upper floor looking towards the little room at the end of the landing. All of a sudden, I clearly heard loud footsteps crossing the wooden floor in the room although I couldn't see anyone through the open door.

My immediate thought was that it must be a colleague who I hadn't realised was in there. I got up to go and talk to whoever it was and as I walked along the short landing the loud footsteps suddenly stopped. In my mind I assumed that whoever it was had walked across the room to look out of the window at the market square below. As I entered the room, I immediately realised there was nobody in there and the only door was the one I had just entered through.

At the time of writing Castle Lodge is no longer open to the public and is in the process of being refurbished by the new owners following the death of Bill Pearson. It was once used as a hotel and the intention now is to turn it into a hotel once again. It will be interesting to see if anything unusual gets reported by any of the guests.

King Charles II Public House

Is the King Charles II pub cellar apparition the most authentic ghost photograph ever taken? The history of this intriguing photograph covers some decades. The author first became aware of it in November 1998 at an ASSAP event in London. Barry Fitzpatrick, from Hereford, had been conducting an impressive long-term investigation into the Charles II public house in Ross-on-Wye in order to obtain Accredited Investigator (AI) status from ASSAP.

King Charles II public house (Chris Whippet, CC BY-SA 2.0)

During the course of this investigation, he had received a pack of photographs which former landlady in the 1970s, Vi Boler, had taken before modifications to the cellar were made. She had said that the gentleman in the pictures was her husband.

In looking through the photographs, Barry spotted the one reproduced here. On the left hand-side a figure can be seen sporting sideburns and what appears to be a drayman's leather apron. He is semi-transparent and has no discernible legs. What is more, he appears to have just passed through the wall. No mention of this strange picture was mentioned when Barry obtained the photographs.

The cellar photograph with the figure against the left hand wall

Accusations of 'obvious fake' and 'photoshopped' were made even back in the late 1990s. Nevertheless, it certainly deserved further investigation. The date given for the picture was around 1973. This was important as it certainly could not have been 'photoshopped' back then. There were two major clues in trying to determine the age. Firstly, the local photography shop who did the processing had stamped their address on the back. It was very faded, but just readable. The address no longer housed the photographers, but they were still in business. They confirmed the date was most likely correct.

Secondly, there are a number of barrels in the cellar which some claimed were too modern for 1973. The author had a good contact on the management team at Banks's Brewery (now Marstons who own the pub). A good quality copy was made and some of the older draymen were asked for an opinion. Unanimously, they agreed that there was nothing in the picture that should not have been there in 1973.

Having dated the picture to our satisfaction, and confirmed it was one of a batch processed by a local photography shop it seemed bizarre to imagine that they would waste time creating an elaborate fake for absolutely no reason. So far, the picture was standing up to scrutiny. However, there were anomalies and some of these were confirmed when we did an investigation at the pub in January 1999. The main problem was light sources that really should not be there. Even accepting that the gentleman might be holding a lamp, the spread of light just does not look right. During our investigation in 1999, we were able to examine the cellar closely. It was difficult to see how the spread of lights coming from the left of the image could have been generated. During the course of our investigation, unexplained flashes of light were seen in the front bar but the infrared camera monitoring the cellar produced nothing of interest.

The photograph was not the only phenomena reported at the pub though. Icy chills and apparitions had been reported above the cellars and also poltergeist type activity with barrels being moved, gas taps getting mysteriously turned off and small items disappearing. More recently, as late as 2017, the landlord went down to the cellar one morning as usual and found the door to be blocked. A bit of pushing got it open enough to squeeze through in order to see what was going on. Unbelievably, a full barrel of beer had been pushed right up to the back of the cellar door blocking it.

The image looked likely to remain an intriguing mystery until photographic expert, Steve Potter, was asked to examine it. Steve was able to painstakingly put together the sequence of events which resulted in the unusual picture. He surmised that in order to photograph the whole cellar with a relatively small flash the photograph was most likely taken using a timed exposure technique also known as 'painting with light'. The camera would have been mounted on a tripod with the shutter left open. The small flash, rather than being mounted on the camera, was handheld and flashed around the cellar to illuminate it. The photographer, Vi's husband, probably thought he was out of camera shot when he squeezed himself up against the cellar wall. In the light of Steve Potter's analysis, it can be seen that the figure is in fact holding up a small flashgun. The reason we only see his upper torso is that the flashlight fails to illuminate his legs so they are not recorded on the film. It seems Vi Boler had been right all along – the gentleman in the pictures was indeed her husband.

Colley Gate, Cradley

A young couple in Colley Gate, we will call them Paul and Nicky, had asked for help when they had begun experiencing various types of activity, but in particular what Nicky described as visits from a 'dark, evil entity'.

On visiting the property, it turned out to be an end of terrace council house and part of a row of six homes. The most obvious feature of the house was right at the end of the medium sized garden. A security fence surrounded a fairly large electricity transformer which could be heard quietly humming so was clearly in use.

Council housing terraced row (John M, CC BY-SA 2.0)

It was Nicky who was sensing what she described as an 'oppressive, evil entity' in her home. This tended to be in the evenings while they were sitting watching the television in the lounge. She would know immediately when the evil entity had entered the room. In addition, Nicky had been suffering from epileptic fits but only since they had moved into the property. These could happen anywhere in the house especially upstairs. Her partner, although very supportive, was not experiencing this even when Nicky said she could actually see the dark figure.

We suspected it was possibly something to do with the proximity of the electricity transformer but needed equipment beyond our means to test this theory out properly. There have been a number of studies into this prompted by the work of Michael Persinger in the 1980s.

Electro-Hypersensitivity (EHS) is recognised in some countries (although not as yet in the UK) as causing all sorts of debilitating conditions and weird effects. The theory is that some people are hypersensitive to the measurable electromagnetic fields generated by most types of electrical equipment. Electromagnetic Field (EMF) meters are commonly used on paranormal investigations. These are generally sensitive to a wide frequency range, do not give accurate readings as they are not calibrated, and are particularly susceptible to interference from other devices such as mobile phones, WiFi routers and a myriad of other sources. Paradoxically, it is these limitations which cause such devices to light up dramatically at the slightest provocation which only seems to add to their popularity.

We sought advice from an acquaintance who was an electrical engineering lecturer at a local college. He was very interested in what we were doing and kindly agreed to loan us an accurate EMF meter. It is important to note that this was an accurate fully calibrated meter designed for measuring EMF strength at 50 Hertz mains frequency which is what we were interested in. Initial baseline readings in fellow investigators' homes showed that readings were negligible unless in close proximity to electrical equipment actually in use.

Three of us had arranged to spend the evening with the couple covering the time the 'dark entity' would be most likely to appear. We deliberately did not give the couple any details of the EMF device, neither did we divulge any readings throughout the evening. To start with, nowhere in the room had a reading of less than 2.5 milligauss. Not significantly high, but certainly more than our own home baseline readings had shown. The device was placed well away from any electrical equipment in the lounge such as the television and left in the same position in order to make comparative readings. These were taken every 10 minutes enabling the graph pictured to be produced. A peak around 8.00 pm coincided with the end of Coronation Street but by far the biggest peak was around 9.00 to 9.30 pm when the room EMF reached nearly 12 milligauss. We would realise later that this was likely due to kettle's going on for a hot drink in between popular TV programmes.

It was at the highest point that Nicky became clearly distressed, announcing that she could see the 'dark entity' and that the atmosphere in the room had become 'oppressive'. Apart from the EMF reading which she did not know about, nothing had changed in the room from our point of view. Very shortly after this, she went into an epileptic fit which her partner was well used by now to coping with. Afterwards, Nicky said the entity had now gone and the atmosphere in the room had gone back to normal. The EMF readings had, by then, also decreased from the high level. At this point we were still assuming that the transformer at the end of the garden was responsible for the high EMF readings, but we were to be proved wrong.

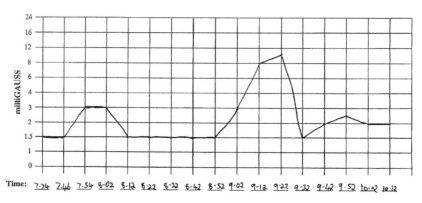

EMF readings taken on the night of our investigation

Having determined the correlation between the EMF readings and what Nicky was experiencing we returned in daylight to try and track down the source. Surprisingly to us, the transformer yielded no EMF readings whatsoever, it was completely and properly shielded. Even more surprising though, the highest readings in the property were taken at the back of the house and these could be traced horizontally across the rear of the building. Assuming that the readings would decrease upstairs we were surprised to find that they were far higher. EMF readings off the scale on our meter were taken in the small bathroom upstairs. In reporting this to the couple it turned out that many of the fits Nicky suffered were indeed in the bathroom where the highest readings were taken.

As an almost last resort to try and solve the mystery of the readings we did a visual check from outside the house in the garden and the answer was right there in plain sight. We had simply been too preoccupied with the transformer to notice. A number of very thick, white covered cables were running under the upstairs window ledges of the entire row of houses. We realised that this was the main electrical supply for the whole row. Instead of coming in at ground level the cables were suspended overhead.

The following week, the local council had arranged to do some electrical work and we of course suggested that they questioned why the mains supply came from upstairs. As it happened, the council removed all of the old mains cabling and replaced it with a conventional ground level supply and electricity meter.

We met up with the couple once more following the electrical work and borrowed the EMF meter once again. This time, all of the readings around the house were as expected. Even better, Nicky had not experienced any more visits from the 'dark entity' and had not suffered any more epileptic fits. When we checked on them a few months later they were about to move to a rural cottage in Wales to live a simpler lifestyle. And who could blame them?

Drakelow - Beneath the Dragon's Mound

Drakelow Tunnels, on Drakelow Lane between Kinver and Wolverley in Worcestershire, is aptly named. Drakelow in Anglo Saxon refers to a 'dragon's mound' or burial ground. Drakelow Tunnels are themselves buried deep into the sandstone beneath Kingsford Country Park. Drakelow and the surrounding area are subject to many reports of alleged paranormal activity. In August 2008, an opportunity presented itself to carry out some research inside the tunnels. Given that at the time this was not at all a well-known location we were interested to see what, if anything, a medium with no previous knowledge of the area would make of it. Quotes used have been taken directly from an audio recording made at the time.

Main entrance concealing nuclear bombproof doors

Drakelow Underground Dispersal Factory began life as a shadow factory for Rover to produce aero engine parts for the Bristol Aeroplane Factory. The tunnels were constructed over the period 1941 to 1942 from a design by

Sir Alexander Gibb and Partners. The initial intention was that aero engine production would be switched to Drakelow should Rover's existing surface factories be bombed into submission. Explosives were used to blast out the 3.5 miles of tunnels and not without serious accidents. One of the worst happened in October 1941, when a roof fall in Tunnel 1 claimed the lives of three men including Harry Depper who is buried locally. Once completed the whole underground area was split between the Rover Shadow Factory and an RAF storage facility for aircraft spares. At the height of its operation men and women would have been working underground producing Mercury and Pegasus aero engine parts. The complex had everything required for working underground including workshops, offices, kitchens, canteens, toilets and even several bars. There was also a concert hall to entertain the wartime workers. In true 1940's style the workers had canteens but the white-collar staff had their own separate dining room. Small battery powered trucks were used to transport materials and finished goods through the network of tunnels. These trucks could move around freely as they were not restricted to running on tracks. In addition to all of this, the RAF also had their separate area of the underground complex where uniformed RAF personnel would have guarded and administered the storage and distribution of essential aircraft spares.

Tunnel 1 where three men lost their lives in a roof fall (Courtesy of Steve Potter)

During the 1960s and through to the early 1990s Drakelow took on the role of a nuclear bomb shelter. Initially designated Regional Seat of Government for Defence Region 9 (RSG9) Drakelow continued to be upgraded throughout the cold war with additions such as nuclear blast proof doors to augment the natural protection from radiation afforded by the sandstone above. In the event of a nuclear war contact would have been maintained with the network of similar Regional Seats of Government throughout the country through a telecommunications system which ran through the complex and a BBC radio broadcasting studio would have provided information to those still left alive outside. Fortunately, Drakelow never needed to be activated for this purpose.

Tunnel 3 by the kitchen and canteen (Courtesy of Steve Potter)

Drakelow Tunnels and the area surrounding it have long been subject to reports of strange phenomena. Whilst investigating an unconnected case an odd sighting was reported to me dating from the winter of 1989 and I was able to interview the principal witness, Michael. He was driving his wife and daughter back home around 11.00 pm at night along Drakelow Lane and had just passed the nuclear bunker on the left. Suddenly finding the car surrounded by a mist, Michael instinctively slammed on his brakes as three figures suddenly appeared crossing the road from right to left. They were not walking but floating through the mist and clearly illuminated by the car's headlights. He described them as being solid looking and wearing dark habits with hoods as if they were monks. However, there is no record of a monastery ever being in the area. Interestingly, the spectre of the three hooded spirits, or Genii Cucullati, is an ancient one which can be traced back to Iron Age, and later Roman Britain. Whilst there was no monastery, there certainly was an Iron Age Celtic hill fort, Solcum Aylesbury, which lies immediately above the Drakelow tunnel complex.

Tunnel 4 near the old Rover offices (Courtesy of Steve Potter)

In the tunnel's themselves 1940's wartime music has sometimes been heard seemingly coming from Tunnel 1. When the source of the music is investigated it abruptly stops. Strange mists have also been seen in the shadow factory part of the complex particularly in and around Tunnel 4. On one occasion a caretaker's two German Shepherds were transfixed by what appeared to be a misty figure in Tunnel 4. The dogs ran off terrified and would not return. People often experience the feeling of being watched and some claim to have been touched or even pushed. One of our guides, Roger, had the experience of seeing a figure he described as a "betrousered leg" disappearing around one of the doorways in a fully lit tunnel. This figure has been given the name 'Oswald' and is purported to have been one of the workers killed during construction of the tunnels. However, there appears to be no evidence to support Oswald as having been a real person and the identities of the two other workers who died along with Harry Depper are not known. Neither are the names of two workers who were tragically mangled to death when they were riding the conveyer belts out of the complex. It is likely that Oswald was named by one of the many ghost hunting groups who have frequently hired the tunnels for investigations. Odd events do continue to occur underground at Drakelow.

The author has been fortunate in being able to investigate the tunnels with small groups of experienced fellow investigators under tightly controlled conditions. On one such investigation with the Stourbridge Independent Paranormal Society everyone in the tunnels at the time had gathered in a tunnel known as 1st Avenue, Government Department. There have been many reports of stones being thrown in this particular area but what we experienced was certainly no stone. This particular tunnel still had the massive metal ventilation ducts suspended from the roof and was not far from a sealed nuclear blast door. We had gathered for a quick update and had just decided to move off into another area. As we did so the whole tunnel shook with an almighty bang. There was no-one anywhere near the area concerned and a thorough search revealed no clue as to what might have happened. It sounded as though the blast door had been slammed shut but this was simply not possible. Fortunately, the event was recorded on the author's headcam. 🎥 1

The idea behind our research was to see what, if anything, someone claiming mediumistic ability might be able to pick up from a location which would give little clue as to its history. We were fortunate in knowing of a medium, Teresa Clarke, who was very interested in being involved in such an experiment. We also had what we considered to be the ideal location in Drakelow Tunnels. Teresa, our medium, did not live locally and would have had no knowledge of the Drakelow tunnel system as at the time (August 2008) fewer people had access, unlike in later years when it was regularly hired out to paranormal groups. That has now come to an end and part of the complex is to become an underground museum. The following is a chronicle of the events that took place during our 2008 investigation.

We had previously agreed that the author would be the only one of our team to contact Teresa in order to limit as far as possible any prior contamination concerning the location. Obviously, transport had to be arranged for Teresa as she could not be told where she was going beforehand. It would be reasonable to assume if inviting someone to an allegedly haunted location they might expect the location to be a house, historic property, pub ,or something similar. Not in this case. One of the first questions Teresa asked was whether the location was safe. In those days, Drakelow was reasonably safe but you still had to be careful where you went. We were to be taken around the site by two experienced local guides. I asked Teresa why she thought it might not be safe. Her impression over the telephone, having been given no clues at all, was of a dark place with things lying around and she asked if it was some sort of factory. Of course, Drakelow had been a shadow factory during World War II. Naturally, I gave no clues whatsoever apart from assuring Teresa that she would be safe and accompanied at all times.

On the night of the investigation, I collected Teresa and we drove the 20 odd miles to Drakelow. The entrance was quite difficult to find especially in the days when the Drakelow Tunnels were less well known. Teresa had no idea where she was. Our little group was shown around by two guides, Roger and Ian, from the Drakelow Preservation Trust which looks after the tunnels.

We entered the tunnel system through the heavy nuclear bomb proof door – a chilling relic of the Cold War. Once inside, the blast door was sealed behind us, and our little group entered the tunnels lit only by the light from our own torches. Teresa immediately felt "almost like I was walking into an aerodrome" and referred to the war (WWII), aircraft and RAF personnel. When Drakelow was a shadow factory it was used to both make aero engine parts and also to store aeroplane spares as Roger later confirmed, "Drakelow would have been occupied by the RAF as a storage area for the RAF. The factory made aero engine parts". RAF personnel would certainly have been here. As well as picking up on male workers Teresa also felt that there were women working down in the tunnels:

Women here working, their hair tied up in scarves … packaging, putting things into boxes … typewriters clicking … quite a few women down here.

At this point we had not seen any ladies toilets which of course would have provided a major clue! Roger confirmed that there would have been women workers including packers in the tool store. Drakelow did not produce complete engines but aero engine parts which would have been packaged. Teresa also had the impression of:

> A cart going up and down on wheels … metal trucks on wheels. Looked like they should be on tracks, but these weren't.

In fact, such a battery powered metal truck was discovered in the tunnels left over from the old WWII shadow factory. Teresa had no knowledge of this when she was giving what was quite a good description of the one remaining electric truck which by this time had in any case been removed.

Remains of WWII poster. Just enough to recognise a Sea Spitfire flying over a British aircraft carrier

After such a promising start we progressed deeper into the complex and Teresa came out with some information which at the time appeared to make no sense. She had the impression of 14-year-old boys being in the tunnels ahead of us, "moving back, about six of them". Teresa described them as wearing, "caps, shirts and braces", suggesting that the boys were connected with the earlier use of the tunnels as a shadow factory. At the time I could think of no reason why 14-year-old boys would have been in the tunnels, but this was to quickly change. Our second guide, Ian, asked me whether I would like to see a part of the tunnels not included in the occasional underground tours. We made our way to a section of the tunnels which I was unable to find on subsequent visits. At one point a very tattered wartime poster was still attached to the wall. There was enough left to later identify it as a propaganda poster showing a Supermarine Sea Spitfire flying over a British aircraft carrier with the caption, 'Great Britain will pursue the WAR AGAINST JAPAN to the very end'. The presence of this poster emphasised the fact that we were very much in the original WWII shadow factory area of the complex.

Further on into the tunnels were some of the original ladies toilets and Ian invited me to go and look at some wartime graffiti still on the wall of the end cubicle. Clearly scrawled here were the words, 'Fancy a boy of fourteen – lovely'. Needless to say, this fitted in perfectly with what Teresa had said about 14-year-old boys being associated with the tunnels. Ian explained that boys generally left school at 14 during the war and some were employed both in the construction and operation of the shadow factory. In fact, children could leave school at 14 up until the 1944 Butler Act which then raised the school leaving age to 15.

World War Two wartime graffiti in the ladies toilets

On rejoining Teresa and the rest of our little group we made our way into Tunnel 1. At one point Teresa suddenly began to feel very uneasy saying that she didn't "like the feeling in this bit". As we went further into this area of the tunnel, she started complaining about feeling a pressure on her back pushing her down. As we carried on, she began to get quite distressed and reluctant to go any further. She was feeling that that there was:

Something falling against me, and I can't push it away … something terrible could have happened down there [pointing to a specific area of the tunnel] … something awful down there.

As we walked past this area Teresa began to feel better and said that the pressure on her back was easing. Without any clue or hint from our guides or anyone else, and after walking a considerable distance through the miles of dark tunnels, Teresa had correctly identified the exact spot where the three workmen digging out Tunnel 1 had been killed in the roof fall of October 1941.

Most if not all that Teresa was able to pick up on referred to the use of Drakelow as a shadow factory during WWII. This is perhaps not surprising as thankfully Drakelow never needed to be made operational as a Regional Seat of Government in the event of a nuclear war.

One of the difficulties in working with a medium is that there is a tendency to recall the things that make sense (the hits) and filter out anything that is wide of the mark (the misses). Added to this there is the possibility of 'cold reading' taking place where information is unintentionally given and picked up on by the medium. To counteract this in our work with Teresa the whole investigation was recorded on two separate devices, one being a backup for the other should we have had any equipment failure. Two things stand out from the recording. Firstly, Teresa is not supplying a continuous stream of information. She relates only what she says she is picking up in different parts of the tunnels. Secondly, the things Teresa does concentrate on (RAF personnel, 14 year old boys, metal trucks and particularly the location of the rock fall) were all descriptions of things we were able to later confirm to her even though the presence of 14-year-old boy workers was only discovered on the night of the investigation itself. All in all, this was a fascinating exercise to be involved with and carried out at a time when knowledge of the Drakelow underground complex was not nearly so much in the public domain as it is now. All credit is due to Teresa Clarke for allowing herself to be tested in this way following the strict protocols imposed by our group.

Of course, it would be erroneous to generalise about mediumistic ability from just this one exercise. It would also be very difficult to reliably replicate today as the possibility of contamination through prior knowledge is that much greater given the explosion of paranormal tourism and public interest in allegedly haunted locations reflected in the plethora of television shows and websites. Replicating such field experiments anyway is notoriously difficult due in part to the number of uncontrolled variables present which could be influencing the results one way or another. However, perhaps the last word is best left to William James commenting on his own work with the medium Leonora Piper:

> If you wish to upset the law that all crows are black, you must not seek to show that no crows are; it is enough if you prove one single crow to be white.

1

Dudley Zoo and Castle

In recent years and encouraged by a visit from the Most Haunted crew, Dudley Castle has been a popular venue for organised ghost hunts. Prior to this, our group was invited by the then Keeper of the Castle, Adrian Durkin, to investigate activity which was causing an issue for a children's entertainer employed during the summer season. There is a very well-known haunting at Dudley Castle, but this activity was something entirely different.

Dudley Castle Keep (Trevman99, CC BY-SA 3.0)

Dudley Castle is home to very possibly the Black Country's most famous ghost – Dorothy Beaumont, the Grey Lady. She was a real person, being the wife of Lieutenant Colonel John Beaumont, Deputy Commander of the Royalist forces during the second siege of Dudley Castle in 1646, during the English Civil War. In 1645, Dorothy had given birth to a daughter, Frances, who sadly died the same year. Frances was buried at St Edmunds Church, known locally as 'bottom church'. In those days, it was common for commanders to order the levelling of buildings prior to a siege to prevent them being used by the enemy. So it was with St Edmunds, which was destroyed on the orders of the Royalist commander, Colonel Leveson. The present day 'bottom church' was rebuilt around 1724.

Dorothy never really recovered from the loss and passed away herself in 1646 during the siege by Sir William Brereton's Parliamentarian forces. Permission was granted by Brereton for Dorothy's body and twelve named mourners to leave the castle so she could be buried at the Church of St Thomas, known locally as 'top church'. She could not be buried with her baby, and neither was her husband allowed to accompany the body.

It is said that Dorothy Beaumont's unquiet spirit still roams the castle grounds around the base of the Keep searching for her baby and husband. More than once on the popular evening ghost walks, visitors at the end have asked why there were two actresses playing the part of the Grey Lady. It seems Dorothy Beaumont herself would sometimes put in a spectral appearance.

The Dudley Castle site plays host to a plethora of ghosts including black robed monks seen in the area around the Undercroft in the castle courtyard. In fact, during one of our investigations at the castle, a dark hooded figure was seen through the stone arch passing across the entrance to the courtyard coming from the direction of the former chapel. The Cluniac monks of the ruined Dudley Priory provided both a place of burial for nobles at the castle and extra accommodation for guests.

Stone arch and entrance to the castle courtyard

A phantom pianist in the Queen Mary Ballroom is only heard when the building is locked up and supposedly empty, although who they might be is not known. A lone figure walking along the top of the battlements on the Keep has been seen on a number of occasions and by credible witnesses. Two police officers investigating a possible intruder decided to check the battlements. One officer climbed up onto the Keep whilst the other remained below in case anyone tried to run away. When he came back down, the other officer demanded to know where the intruder was. It seems that from below, two figures were visible walking along the battlements. The officer up on the Keep had seen nothing unusual.

An anniversary ghost is also said to haunt the Keep. Legend has it that an old woman lived there and either hung herself from the top of the Keep or else was thrown off. Either way, she is said to re-enact the grisly spectacle each Halloween. A group on a charity ghost hunt had a similar experience to the police officers when they watched a figure walking up and down the top of the Keep. Despite it being a ghost hunt, nobody volunteered to go up and see who or what was up there!

There are many such stories but Chris Jeans, the children's entertainer 'Bonkers the Clown', was losing sleep due to regular night-time disturbances. He was being put up for the summer in the Castle Lodge situated on the perimeter of the zoo grounds near the entrance. This quirky little building was built around 1900 and is better known as the 'Round House' although it is not really round. The author was able to interview Chris Jeans and obtain his story first hand:

Chris explained that his sleep was being regularly interrupted by loud bangs coming from within the building. He would see misty figures on the stairs up to his bedroom and sometimes in the early hours someone would be violently rattling the front door trying to get in. When he looked there was never anybody there. This was bad enough, but the final straw was the ghost that appeared at the bottom of his bed. The apparition was that of a middle-aged man who Chris could see quite clearly. He was visible only from the waist up and had no discernible legs. Unusually, the apparition spoke and said to Chris, "Why have you returned?". Enough was enough, and this experience frightened him so much that Chris took to sleeping in his car.

At the same time as Chris Jeans was experiencing his disturbed nights, one of the castle's cleaners, Christine Bullas, had a most unusual sighting in the Undercroft, which was once part of the old chapel in the castle courtyard. This is home to two stone coffins, the larger of which was moved from the nearby Dudley Priory and is said to have once held the body of John de Somery. He was the so-called 'Bad Baron' of Dudley Castle who thought nothing of robbery and murder to further his own ends.

Dudley Castle Sharrington Range in the Courtyard with the Undercroft to the right

Christine was working in the Undercroft early one morning when she looked up to see a pair of medieval looking knee length boots standing up in the larger coffin. As she stared in disbelief they gradually faded away. Another cleaner, again working early in the morning, was in what used to be the Tropical House. Through the window she was surprised to see a little girl in a simple brown dress just standing and staring at her. The cleaner glanced away for a second but when she looked back the little girl was gone.

With such activity going on, there was great interest in investigating the castle. In fact, a total of ten investigations were held here over some five years. On our initial investigation we were naturally keen to investigate the Round House which seemed to be the centre of the activity at the time, at least as far as Chris Jeans was concerned. Around midnight, the author and three other investigators were scheduled to be down in the Round House.

The Castle Lodge better known as the 'Round House'

It was our first time in the Round House, and we were surprised how small it actually was. From the living space downstairs, a short staircase led up to the bedroom above. Three investigators positioned themselves downstairs whilst I sat at the top of the stairs. As the reported experiences had been in the dark, we turned off the lights and waited. After about twenty minutes the silence was shattered by an almighty bang. It came from downstairs and was definitely inside the building. It sounded as though something very heavy had been pushed over or dropped. We turned the lights on, and it was immediately obvious that nothing in the tiny building had moved or fallen, let alone make such a huge bang. We could find no explanation at all for what we had all just witnessed.

Despite other groups covering the Round House throughout the night, the bang we had heard was not repeated. On a subsequent investigation, the door to the Round House was heard to be rattled violently from outside. There was nobody there.

In the castle courtyard a long passageway ran through the ruined Sharrington Range leading to a display area and then out through a shop. This whole area was regularly subject to the sounds of doors opening and closing, loud footsteps, and whispered voices. The source of these sounds which were clearly heard could never be determined. Similarly, outside in the courtyard the author also heard a woman's voice coming from the Sharrington Range:

> A temporary stage had been set up against the Sharrington Range where once stone steps led up towards the Great Hall. High up on the left-hand side I could hear someone talking. Although it was clearly a woman, it wasn't possible to tell what she was saying. Other than the ground floor, there is no safe access to the ruins above except that I managed to get closer by climbing up onto the stage. Even so, although the voice could still be heard, it was simply not possible for anyone to be up there. By the time anyone else arrived, the voice had ceased.

This area is very close to the shop where, on the same investigation, a woman was clearly heard saying, "Look at this". Over the years, there have been a number of photographs taken which appear to show a woman in period dress in different parts of the ruined Sharrington Range.

Dudley College Broadway Site

Theme is no better way to investigate a site on a long-term basis than to actually work there as the author did for many years. Whilst much of the extensive campus in Dudley is modern, the original Broadway site dates back to 1936 when it was first opened to students. The Broadway site is situated between the Priory Ruins and Dudley Castle. This whole area of Dudley is renowned for reports of paranormal activity and the Broadway Campus is no exception.

Dudley College Broadway Site

Over a period of many years there have been numerous reports of alleged paranormal activity within the College buildings. There are three main floors designated *A*, *B* and *C* with *A* floor being the lower ground. In addition, *E* block, which is not physically connected to the main building, has also been the source of reported activity.

The main entrance is on *B* floor and it is here, usually at night, that the sound of keys jangling is heard. Older members of staff who remember him, put this down to a long-deceased caretaker who used to live on site in a flat situated on the roof. Apparently, when he walked around he always jangled his large set of college keys. There have also been sightings of a shadowy figure described as a monk on this floor although it has to be noted this may have been influenced by the proximity of the Priory Ruins behind the main block. A less shadowy figure has been described as a slight, dapper gentleman who has been seen, including by the author, around the refectory area of *B* floor.

The ruined Dudley Priory immediately behind the college

In 2004, some workers employed to do a job on *A* floor, over the weekend whilst the college was closed, were greatly disturbed when the goods lift started operating on its own. Although the lift was later checked, no fault could be found. It had apparently been going up and down between *A* floor and the top of the building which used to be the old caretaker's flat.

Moving on to *C* floor, doors open and close on their own, footsteps have been heard crossing empty wooden floors and faces have been seen peering through classroom windows when there is nobody there. When the building opened in the 1930s, the old laundry was situated on the ground floor of *E* Block. The area was later used for storage but very often the sound of a lady or girl singing could be heard coming from this area although the exact source could never be determined.

Whilst working at the Broadway site, on two separate occasions the author experienced some of this paranormal activity.

In my late teens I was given the job of installing a local telephone system between two rooms in the middle of a long corridor on *C* floor. This was to be used for examinations by the Office Studies Department. The idea was that the examiner would be in one room out of sight of the student in the room next door. It was a holiday period and there were few people in the building let alone where I was working. Having drilled through and connected the telephones I lifted the handset in the room I was in to test the connection. It was lunch time, and I was expecting my colleague to come up so we could go to lunch. As I had the handset to my ear, I heard him open the door and walk across the room next door towards the phone. I decided to surprise him and moved quickly out into the corridor and pushed open the door to the next classroom. There was nobody there. The classroom and the corridor were both deserted. When I finally caught up with him, he had not even been up on *C* floor.

This was unusual in itself, but it was by no means the end of the story. At the time, *C* floor was divided up between a corridor of rooms for office studies and a similar corridor with science laboratories. I happened to mention my experience to one of the science technicians and he demanded to know who I had been talking to. I managed to convince him that it was my own experience and the whole story came out. The science technicians had their own little rooms attached to the main science laboratories. They had virtually all had the same experience of hearing the classroom door open and someone walking across the room when there was nobody there, usually when it was quiet such as in the holiday periods. Of course, these were science technicians so perhaps understandably they didn't particularly want to be talking openly about something that had no rational explanation.

The second experience came many years later when the author was employed on a national educational project but based in what was then the Special Needs Department at the Broadway site.

The job involved attending a lot of conferences around the country and on one particular occasion, I had left my lecture notes in the room I used on *B* floor. It was an early start and I decided to call at the Broadway site to pick them up first. It was about 7.30 am but I knew the building would be open as the cleaning staff would have already started. I made my way to the long corridor leading to the rear of *B* floor past the staff dining room and the student refectory. The Special Needs rooms were at the end of this corridor with *B* 15 on the right. The long corridor ended in a left-hand bend at the end of the building. Up to this point I had not seen anybody else in the building. As I walked past the refectory, I clearly saw a small, dapper looking chap in a dark suit come around the bend at the end of the corridor and go straight into Room *B* 15. One particular thing I noticed about him was his rather old fashioned looking rectangular leather briefcase.

Now it so happened that our small kitchen area was in *B* 15 and over the past few weeks we had been having coffee go missing. My first thought was that here was the culprit! *B* 15 only had one entrance and so there was nowhere the man could go. I slowed down in order to catch him red handed helping himself to our coffee. As I approached the double classroom doors he still hadn't come out. Fully expecting to confront the coffee thief in I went. There was nobody there. The room was empty and there was absolutely nowhere the dapper little man could have gone or could be hiding.

The room in question was used to teach mining engineering up until the 1960s when the last deep coal mine in the area, Baggeridge, was shut down. The long-deceased mining lecturer, Sam Thompson, matched the description of the phantom figure with the briefcase. Apparently, he always used to arrive early for work to prepare for the day's lessons.

This was the incident, more than any other, which sparked the author's interest in ghosts and hauntings. Following these events and many others, an overnight investigation in 2004 was organised between Parasearch and interested staff. Experienced investigators led small teams for 45-minute vigil sessions in predesignated areas of the college. Between 9.00 pm and 3.00 am the vigil teams circulated around each of the main floors and *E* Block. Lots of bumps and bangs, some quite loud, were recorded all over the building although much of this can probably be put down to the building settling.

Of much more interest was a dark figure entering room C 14. This was clearly observed by one of the investigators and on inspecting the room, the door was found to be locked. Perhaps the most interesting event of the evening though occurred in E Block. One of the vigil teams reported hearing a lady quietly singing and coming from the area which used to be the College laundry although the exact source could not be identified. Vigil teams were not briefed beforehand on what to expect, or indeed what phenomena had been reported on the Broadway Site prior to this investigation.

Gibbet Lane

The area around what is now called Gibbet Lane used to be called Fir Tree Hill. The events of December 12th 1812, would ensure that this once pleasant wooded lane would never be seen in the same light again. The track that is now Gibbet Lane was what passed for a road in 1812. Gentleman farmer Benjamin Robins had enjoyed a good day at Stourbridge market and was making his way home to Dunsley Hall, carrying over £20 which was a considerable amount in those days.

The area around Fir Tree Hill now known as Gibbet Lane

Unbeknownst to Robins his success that day had not gone unnoticed by one William Howe, a self-styled highwayman. Robins became aware of Howe walking briskly some way behind him on the otherwise deserted track. Fully expecting a few words of greeting when Howe caught up with him, Robins was totally unprepared for what happened next. Without saying a word, Howe took out an old pistol and shot Robins in the back at point blank range. He fell to the floor mortally wounded but did not die straight away. After being robbed of his money and a fine silver pocket watch, Robins managed to crawl the last half a mile or so home. He lingered between life and death for ten days but died of his wound ten days later on the 28th of December.

Dunsley Hall Hotel the former home of Benjamin Robins

People in Stourbridge were outraged that this should happen to such a respected local gentleman farmer. So much so, money was raised locally in order to pay for a pair of Bow Street runners from London to investigate the case and bring the perpetrator to justice. This was in the days before the formation of a proper police force, but Bow Street Runners were available for hire at a price. Harry Adkins and Samuel Taunton mounted a thorough investigation and eventually apprehended Howe who had tried to escape to London after pawning the silver pocket watch. Howe was a local farm hand who fancied himself as a highwayman, albeit without a horse as he could not afford one. He was imprisoned awaiting trial at Stafford Gaol. It was here that Howe made his biggest mistake and sealed his fate. He had hidden one of his pair of old pistols in a hayrick at Oldswinford and wrote to his wife telling her to find and dispose of the incriminating weapon. He should have known his wife could not read. She had to get someone else to read the letter and the game was up. That, and the testimony from pawnbroker Edward

Power of Warwick, ensured that Howe was sentenced to hang. Not only that, but his body was to be gibbeted from a tree at the scene of his crime. In fact, William Howe, was one of the last prisoners to be gibbeted in England before the gruesome practice was abolished. After execution, his body was placed in an iron frame, the gibbet, and hung from a tree on Fir Tree Hill. It was intended as a dire warning to others, but clearly it did not work as a local newspaper estimated that upwards of 40,000 people visited the site on the first weekend that Howe was gibbeted, and the whole affair took on a 'carnival' atmosphere. Not so for the family of Benjamin Robbins though, who could see the rotting corpse from one of the windows in Dunsley Hall. They had the window bricked up.

Illustrated Police News of Saturday 14th December 1872
(Courtesy of the British Library)

The gibbet was there for approximately 18 months and then mysteriously disappeared. Some say a local Doctor took the skeleton, but this is unlikely as after this amount of time there would not have been too much left.

Another theory is that the gibbet was taken down and the iron used to make a gate. What little was left of Howe was reported to have been buried under the tree where he was gibbeted, with a dagger plunged through where his heart would have been. The idea was to keep his unquiet spirit in the ground where it belonged. Clearly this did not work.

The Brierley Hill and Stourbridge Advertiser of December 1872 carried a report from a local gentleman who claimed to have encountered the ghost of William Howe on what was now called Gibbet Lane. The ghost glided up to the gentleman and blocked his path with a menacing laugh. The gentleman instinctively lashed out with his stick to defend himself. The stick passed right through the ghost of Howe and the gentleman, now knocked off his feet, ended up in the ditch. Howe reared up and refused to let the gentleman get up until the first light of dawn, when he suddenly disappeared with a 'blood freezing chuckle'.

In the 1940s a lady walking home one night along Gibbet Lane was stalked by the 'silhouette' of a man she could see following her in the moonlight. Thankfully for her he disappeared as soon as he reached the tree where the gibbet had been. The lady described the man as having a head that flopped from side to side as he walked as if his neck was snapped.

Even today, Gibbet Lane has a sinister feeling about it even on a nice summer's day. People claim to see a dark figure watching them from the trees and the sound of clanking iron has been heard around the site of the gibbet.

The author has investigated the site on a number of occasions, and can confirm the sinister feeling of being watched but during one such investigation:

> We had split up and the author with another investigator were standing near where we believed the gibbet to have been. We both heard what appeared to be the sound of ironwork creaking in the light breeze. There was nothing around us except for trees and bushes – certainly nothing that could have been responsible for making such a noise which lasted for a good few seconds before stopping.
>
> We waited for some time afterwards hoping the clanking sound would return but of course it didn't. Despite subsequent visits we never heard the sound again and a follow up visit in daylight confirmed that there was nothing anywhere near the spot that could possibly have been responsible for making the sound of clanking iron.

Graftonbury Garden Hotel

April 2003 saw a number of paranormal investigators invited to the Graftonbury Garden Hotel in Herefordshire to look into ongoing activity there. This lovely old building started life as a Victorian country residence around 1870, but by the 1960s had been turned into a popular hotel.

Graftonbury Garden Hotel (Chris Shaw, CC BY-SA 2.0)

At the time we went the building was experiencing poltergeist type activity in the bar but mainly in the dining room and an abandoned flat upstairs. Staff would lay out the plates and cutlery ready for evening dinner or breakfast service only to find the placings rearranged when they knew nobody had been anywhere near. Some staff also claimed to have seen the ghost of a little boy in the building who may have been responsible for the mischievous rearranging of the place settings.

Another area of poltergeist activity was a flat which had been added to the top of the building but was now in a derelict state. Movement noises and bangs would be heard coming from the empty flat on occasions. At some point in time, although we could not determine when, it had suffered from fire damage. The flat was accessed by a very narrow stairway situated at the end of the corridor on the upper floor of the hotel. Our investigation centred mainly on the bar, dining room and rooftop flat.

For this investigation we were trialling a new video camera setup using a portable transmitter which could be securely attached to a belt. The receiver with a monitor and video recorder was set up in a nearby empty bedroom. Initial tests along the corridor and on the stairs proved that everything was working as it should.

Hopes were high for the flat as two investigators had already experienced movement noises in there but had not seen anything. For our session in there it was decided that my colleague, Mark, would look after the video recording setup whilst I took the camera up into the flat. The transmitter came with a secure belt clip and was connected to the handheld camera via power and video leads.

I made my way up into the flat up the steep stairs. The door opened into a fairly large room with a further smaller room to the left which I assumed to have once been the bedroom. The flat was very derelict and mostly devoid of furniture. It was in total darkness as there was no longer any mains power supply up there, but the video camera had infrared lights and I had my torch. Having looked around the living room I stepped into the adjoining bedroom.

I didn't see anything but suddenly felt the transmitter being wrenched forcefully from my belt and heard it being thrown across the room. It landed on the wooden floorboards some feet away from me and then flat was silent again. I hoped that this sudden and totally unexpected event had been recorded on the video downstairs. There was nothing else to do except gather up the equipment and make my way back down to the base room.

It turned out that on entering the flat the signal from the camera had become very patchy with lots of static. The signal had been lost altogether as soon as the bedroom was entered. The transmitter had survived being thrown across the room, but we did notice something curious with the connecting lead. It now had a tight knot in it which had definitely not been there when we set the equipment up.

The obvious thing to do was reattach the equipment and try again. This time everything worked perfectly and despite repeating the walk around the flat and the bedroom we simply could not replicate the original event. The rest of the investigation passed off without any further significant incidents.

Despite much deliberation and experimentation, we could find no logical reason why a securely clipped transmitter should suddenly detach itself. The clip wasn't broken and not only that, even if it had somehow managed to come off my belt it certainly wouldn't have landed on the other side of the bedroom.

Update: The flat no longer exists and the whole building has now been transformed into luxury flats.

Graisley Old Hall

When an opportunity arose to investigate Graisley Old Hall (also spelt Graiseley) in Pennfields, Wolverhampton we jumped at the chance. In more recent times it has become very popular with commercial ghost hunting groups although it is privately owned and not normally open to the public. It is one of the oldest residential buildings in Wolverhampton dating back to at least the 15th century.

Graisley Old Hall

In 2002, the house hit the headlines for poltergeist activity and the BBC named it 'The house that cries'. This was a reference to the anomalous appearances of water dripping from one of the beams in the main hall. This might not seem so unusual in such an old house, but the owner was able to confirm that the dripping water was not leaking from anywhere on the ground floor or the floor above. What is more, the water and any wetness would disappear as quickly as it appeared, leaving no trace. Pools of water are often associated with poltergeist cases, and it seems the outbreak in 2002 was by no means the first experienced in the house. In the 1930s, the house was owned by the Royal Wolverhampton School. From this period onwards there were rumours of spasmodic outbreaks of poltergeist activity although it is not known if this included pools of water.

Common practice when ships were made of wood was to salvage timbers and use them in house construction. Some such timbers have been identified at Graisley Old Hall. There is no way of knowing whether the water that appeared was salty or not, but it would have been interesting to find out given the connection to the sea through the timbers.

Unfortunately, during our investigation there was no sign of water leaks, anomalous or otherwise, but the building was certainly active particularly in the early hours of the morning. Throughout the investigation we had divided into groups of two or three in order to cover as many of the rooms as possible. From the outside, the house does not look that large but inside there are a surprising number of rooms including a corridor of bedrooms on the first floor.

Bedroom nearest the staircase

Whilst the author and a colleague were in the room nearest to the staircase, we heard someone come up the wooden stairs and onto the landing outside. Naturally, we assumed this to one of our team who had come upstairs for some reason. This was not the case. Not only was there nobody outside on the landing or in the corridor when we looked, but none of our small team had moved from their allocated areas. Throughout the investigation, group members were reporting hearing the sounds of someone moving around. Every time this was checked there was nobody there, and none of our team had moved.

The final confirmation of this came at the end of the investigation when we were all gathered in the hall by the stairs preparing to leave. Somebody said, "Who is still upstairs?". The answer was nobody as we were all together. We immediately stopped talking to listen and sure enough the sound of someone walking around upstairs on the wooden floor could be clearly heard. As the stairs were the only way down, we listened for a short while before going upstairs to check. Of course, there was nobody there and we could find no clue as to who or what might have been walking around up there.

Gresley Old Hall

Gresley Old Hall in Swadlincote, South Derbyshire has a long reputation for being haunted although there appears to be no actual ghost story associated with it. The house has been much changed over the years but originally dates back to 1556 when Sir Christopher Alleyne had it built allegedly out stone from the ruins of Gresley Priory. This seems most unlikely as the original building was wood although the stone in the original fireplaces could well have come from the Priory. This rather vague connection may explain why the ghosts of monks have allegedly been seen in the area.

A major rebuilding of the house in brick took place around 1700. It was restored again before the Second World War and eventually purchased by The National Coal Board in 1953. It was leased to the Miners' Welfare Club which explains why the old hall is attached to a social club.

In stark contrast to the warm and comfortable social club next door, when we investigated in January 2016 the hall itself was cold and bare, with shutters on many of the windows making it feel dark and oppressive. No wonder then that it has such a reputation for being haunted. The wind was really howling most of the time we were there, adding to the atmosphere of the place. As well as the monks, light anomalies have been reported inside the building as we would later be able to confirm. The ghost of an old lady, possibly a servant, has also been seen together with an entity described only as a dark shape.

> During our investigation we split up into pairs to investigate the many rooms. One of our vigil sessions was in a former bedroom off the first-floor landing. This room was in complete darkness apart from our torches. The author was wearing a headcam, with an infrared light for illumination and a small video recorder with an LCD monitor. We were standing towards the rear of the room. To our left was another smaller room which was empty. The outside window to this room was boarded up. In front of us on the right-hand side was the door which led out onto the landing and another bedroom on the opposite side. There was a small amount of light coming from the door, so it was possible to make out the landing even though our room was dark. We were due to spend 45 minutes in the bedroom before moving to the next location. With just a few minutes to go we were beginning to think of moving on when something caught our eye to the left of the door. We confirmed that we were both seeing the same thing. A vertical strip of pure white light was moving from left to right where the floor meets the wall. We watched it for a few seconds before it disappeared by the door. The light was accompanied by what looked like an amorphous black shadow which also passed from left to right and was seen most clearly in the doorway.

We thoroughly investigated possible sources for the light and the shadow but could find none. If anything, the headcam footage was a bit disappointing. The white light which we both clearly saw was drowned out by the infrared illuminator and did not appear at all on the footage. The shadow though can just be seen in the doorway. 🎥 1 At least we managed to record something.

🎥 1

Guy's Cliffe

Guy's Cliffe in Warwickshire is the archetypal haunted house although this is partly due to Granada Television who managed to burn it down in 1992. Whilst filming an episode of The Case-Book of Sherlock Holmes entitled The Last Vampyre, a stunt went disastrously wrong, and what was supposed to be a controlled fire got out of hand and destroyed what was left of the old building.

Impressive entrance to Guy's Cliffe

The legendary Guy of Warwick and the ghost of the lovely Lady Felice is on a par with the legends of King Arthur and Robin Hood but not as well known. Guy of Warwick first appears in 13th century romances, but his story is set in the 10th century.

Guy is a low born page but falls in love with the Earl of Warwick's lovely daughter Felice. In order to make a name for himself, he sets off to perform heroic deeds such as killing the monstrous, but mythical, Dun Cow which was terrorizing Warwickshire. This and other deeds were not enough though and in order to achieve knightly fame sets off into Europe. After many battles he returns triumphant and marries Felice. Unfortunately, he is overcome by guilt for his actions and sets off again, this time for the Holy Land disguised as a pilgrim. Here, he rights many wrongs before returning again to England only to find King Athelstan in desperate need of a knight to fight the Danes' champion Colbron.

This he does in a fierce battle and returns to Felice still disguised as a pilgrim. She does not recognise him, and he takes up residence in a nearby cave to live the life of a hermit. Shortly before death he sends his gold ring to Felice who rushes to his side just before he dies. In one version of the story Lady Felice dies of a broken heart one month after Guy and in another she flings herself grief stricken from the cliff that gives the house its name. Since then, Guy's Cliffe has become well known for its many stories of ghosts and hauntings including the Lady Felice herself who has allegedly been seen from time to time re-enacting her tragic death leap.

The ruin that is Guy's Cliffe

Built on a sandstone outcrop high above the River Avon, the once magnificent 18th century Palladian style house is now a ruin. The Chapel and the few remaining rooms still in use are now leased to the Freemasons.

Despite the Guy of Warwick story being mainly myth there is still the remains of a hermitage cave below the house together with later caves dug out of the sandstone. Opposite the house a whole series of caves with wooden door fronts have been cut out culminating in a massive stable at the end of the drive. The sandstone forms a natural barrier so there is only one way in and out of these chambers. Guy's Cliffe is a fascinating mix of ruined house, cellars, chapel, caves, and Masonic Lodge.

Top of the drive where the figure was seen from

Apart from the medieval story of the ghost of Felice, there have been many reports of paranormal activity all over the site. Low level poltergeist activity has been experienced, in particular stone throwing which is a fairly common phenomenon. Footsteps, tapping and loud inexplicable bangs are also heard. There are visual effects with flashes, streaks, and odd swirls of light. Dark figures are seen moving around all over the building. In particular, as we discovered on the night of our investigation, the figure of a man had recently been seen crossing from the direction of the chapel and heading towards the stable. We should have set up an outside camera.

During the investigation odd tapping sounds were noted particularly in the Chapel area coming from one particular corner. No logical explanation for this could be found. However, it was when Steve Willis and the author went outside that things really started to get interesting.

> It was our turn to go outside for a 45-minute vigil session We had decided to have a slow walk up to the top of the drive to get a closer look at some of the ruins. The rest of the group were in designated areas either inside the main building, down in the outside cellar or in the large stable. There should not have been anybody else outside at the time. When we reached the top Steve was looking in one of the ruined buildings when I turned to look back down the driveway. A fairly weak external night light was on and just as I turned a figure looking like a man walked from the direction of the Chapel on the left towards the stable. It was far too distant to make out any detail except that it looked like a man. The buildings on the right were all locked up and only the stable was open for our investigation. As we walked back down we were able to ensure that nobody walked back across the drive. On reaching the stable, the man had to have gone in as there was absolutely nowhere else he could have gone. The heavy stable doors were closed with one of our groups positioned inside.
>
> As I reached the doors the left one started to open for me. I assumed one of the team was pushing it from the inside. It turned out not to be the case. As we went inside, we could see that the group were sitting together towards the rear of the stable. Nobody had come in or gone out and what is more nobody had got up to push the door open and they couldn't have seen us coming anyway. A check with our other groups and the caretaker confirmed that nobody had been outside apart from Steve and myself.

As the author was wearing a headcam, expectations were high that this whole episode had been video recorded. Unfortunately, we were simply too far away to record the man on the driveway. However, the video recording does indeed show that the stable door was opening by itself just as I approached it. 🎥 1

The stable is effectively a massive cave with very heavy wooden doors. It required a good push to open it at all and at no other time during our investigation there did it move. Speaking to the caretaker afterwards, he was not at all surprised that this figure had been seen. There is no clue as to who he might be or indeed why he should appear in the stable area.

🎥 1

Halesowen Poltergeist

One of the problems with poltergeist type activity is that it tends to be short lived. By the time witnesses have got around to finding someone to contact the activity has often subsided. Poltergeist activity tends to escalate before suddenly dying out altogether. Typical reported activity often starts with scratching and tapping noises. This might be followed by footsteps and doors opening and closing. At its peak, items might appear or disappear and, in some cases, small items such as stones or coins might get thrown by unseen hands.

A poltergeist is a 'noisy spirit' or more accurately translated from the German a 'rumbling' or 'knocking' spirit. It is sometimes, although not always, associated with children or teenagers. The name sums up these types of manifestations quite well. Typically, in these sorts of cases the activity is rarely witnessed but the results certainly are. Even where something is thrown, whoever or whatever is doing the throwing is rarely if ever seen. Because poltergeist activity involves physical effects any investigation has to start with looking for a natural explanation for the phenomena.

A case in Stourbridge provides a good example. A lady had moved into a Victorian industrial building which had been converted to flats. Whilst in bed at night she would regularly hear someone walking unseen across her bedroom floor. Unnerving to say the least. An examination of the flat revealed that the floorboards in the bedroom appeared to pass under what was clearly a new partition wall. The floorboards did indeed pass under the wall and across a corridor into another flat opposite. We were able to demonstrate, much to her relief, that anyone walking in the corridor, and presumably in the flat opposite as well, would sound as if they were walking across her bedroom floor. This is not as uncommon as it may sound particularly with buildings which have been converted into multiple flats.

One middle aged couple in a house just outside Halesowen were experiencing a range of typical poltergeist activity which seemed to have reached a peak when we were called in. The activity was taking place upstairs in a perfectly ordinary three-bedroom house on a quiet residential estate. Things would be moved around in the bedrooms, bumps and bangs would be heard from above when the couple were downstairs but would cease immediately they went to check. A particular focus for the activity seemed to be a fine antique oak cupboard on the upstairs landing. Very often on getting up in the morning the doors would be flung wide open. After noting down the details from the couple we did what we always do in such cases and asked them to keep a detailed diary of any activity, noting down the date, time, and details of any further events.

Before leaving we were shown around upstairs to see where all the activity was taking place. Examination of the cupboard revealed no obvious reasons why the doors should be opening on their own. They were quite heavy and could not be made to swing out of their own accord even if deliberately opened a little way. Everything seemed very normal until we were shown into the main front bedroom and smaller bedroom. It can best be described as entering a walk-in freezer. It felt absolutely chilling whereas the other bedroom, landing, and indeed the rest of the house was comfortably warm. The couple showing us around made no mention of the sudden temperature drop so we didn't mention it either for fear of making matters worse. Disturbingly, the smaller bedroom was where their child slept.

Once we were back in the car, I asked my colleague what he thought of the extreme temperature drop. It turned out that he had not experienced any cold in the rooms at all. In fact, he commented that the whole house had just felt comfortably warm. Needless to say, we were interested to return with some equipment to do a proper investigation.

As per usual in such cases a follow up phone call was made a week later to check on how things were going. It turned out that there had been no further activity to the great relief of the couple concerned. They said they would get back in touch if anything else happened. In the event, we never heard from them again and can only assume that the activity had ceased.

This was not at all unusual with outbreaks of poltergeist type activity. They are notoriously short lived and prone to suddenly ceasing and never to recur. From experience, it also seems that getting witnesses to take some control of the situation by diligently recording the details of any occurrences would often contribute to putting a stop to the activity. Although anecdotal, this happened time and again with all sorts of anomalous phenomena and not just poltergeists.

Hawthorn Retirement Home

When the owner asked us to investigate some disturbing phenomena regularly occurring in her privately run retirement home, we were asked not to divulge the names of the people involved or the actual location. This was perfectly understandable as the location was a working retirement home in the Black Country at the time we investigated. Hawthorn Retirement Home remains to this day one of the most active locations we have ever investigated with a wide range of phenomena being reported by multiple witnesses. An apparition observed by the author later revealed a tragic story which was not known at the start of the case. Fellow investigator, Dennis Bache, was also witness to some remarkable phenomena.

Hawthorn Retirement Home

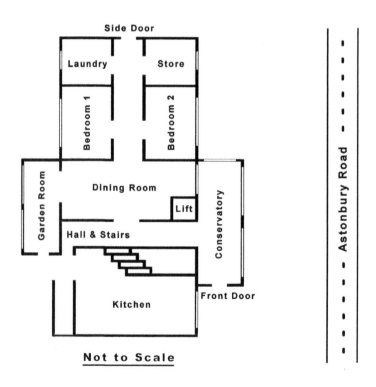

Plan of the areas where the majority of the phenomena had been reported

The Hawthorn Retirement Home was converted from a large, detached house. The property was built around 1952 by a local garage owner on former farmland. From 1960 it had been the home of a Doctor, and also used as the surgery until 1984. It was then purchased by Margaret and her husband Harold as a family home before being turned into a retirement home. At the time of our investigation the residential home had 18 aged and infirm residents looked after by 24 staff.

An extraordinary range of phenomena was being reported here. Over a series of investigations, we were able to record experiences from different members of staff although we had no direct contact with any of the residents who were all old and infirm. It seems the activity had all started around Bedroom 2 and one of the first residents. This lady had long hair which she used to pin up in a knot with long, open pins. These pins would still keep turning up long after the resident had passed away.

The activity we were called in for had started with a resident saying she could hear lovely music playing although nobody else could – at first that is. As time went on members of staff also started hearing the music. It was described as lovely choral music and seemed to be coming from the storeroom behind Bedroom 2 although there was no logical reason for this. From then on, the music was heard regularly by staff and residents, but the source could never be found.

Staff also began experiencing the strong smell of tobacco even though the building was strictly non-smoking, and any smoking would have set off the fire alarms. There was also the strong smell of floral perfume, described by those who smelt it as 'old fashioned'. These smells would be very strong for a few seconds and then just suddenly disappear.

Things then took a more sinister turn when music described as 'a dark funeral sound' was heard. By this time things were escalating, and staff would hear their names being called. Disembodied voices would say, 'Hello Anne' or 'Hello Val'. We asked if anyone had tried to record any of this, but they were instructed not to after two members of staff had tried an experiment one night to try and discover who was responsible.

Most of the activity was in the area of the corridor off the lounge and around Bedroom's 1 and 2. As well as the music, fleeting, dark shadows were now being seen all over the building but particularly in the dining room area. According to Val and Anne the shadows would suddenly appear and just as quickly disappear rather than fading in and out. Val described the figures as seen, "from the head down, sometimes just from the head to the knees, sometimes from the feet to the shoulders. Occasionally you can see the full shapes". On occasions, pairs of shadow figures would be seen moving together.

It should be noted that there are various non-paranormal explanations for 'shadow ghosts'. However, here we had brightly lit rooms and most unusually both staff on duty at night would watch the shifting shadows together.

It wasn't long before more than shadows were being seen. In the corner of the Dining Room was a lift to the upper floor with a small glass window. Coming down one night Val had the unnerving experience of seeing a face looking in at her from the dining room. Val didn't recognise who it was, and the face had disappeared by the time the lift door was opened. Next to be seen was Joyce, a former resident. This time it was Anne who saw her from inside the kitchen. Joyce was seen again sitting in the dining room but this time by night staff Marie and Dot. She was dressed in white and appeared long enough for Marie to recognise who it was. She remembered her from before she passed away.

Another remarkable sighting took place at approximately two in the morning when Val was alone in the dining room. She saw the figure of an old woman in a green striped dress come through the wall of the extension which used to be part of the garden. The figure, which looked solid, floated towards Val just off the floor and stroked her cheek. Val described the woman as being about 80 years of age, under 5ft (1.5m) tall, with rounded unsmiling features, very pale skin, and white hair. Val described the sensation of being stroked as being soft and 'normal'. The apparition then disappeared suddenly, 'out like a light' according to Val. Other members of staff also reported the sensation of having their faces or hair gently stroked by an unseen hand. This sensation was often preceded by a feeling of freezing cold even though the home is always kept warm.

Val could not identify the figure at the time. However, the following Christmas she recognised the figure she had seen in a photo album of residents. It turned out to be a woman called Emily who had passed away before Val was employed at the home. Harold confirmed that when Emily was alive the extension had not yet been built and she would have been walking in the garden area at the rear of the building. Margaret remembered that Emily's favourite dress was indeed green striped.

Residents had been frightened by figures seen in both Bedroom's 1 and 2. Shortly before we were called in to investigate, a resident in Room 1 had become hysterical after seeing a 'fella' standing in the corner of her room. When Val and Anne went to help a former resident of Room 2 to get to bed, she started shouting, "Tell him to go". She was assured it was only Anne. "No, not Anne, him stood next to Anne'. Another resident, a gentleman, said to a member of staff one evening, "You've got something here that shouldn't be here". The member of staff said she pretended she did not know what he meant. He said, "I don't mind, but I object when they try and push me out of bed". His little dog was apparently in the chair at the time looking scared! According to Margaret, there were also instances of the dining room chairs and cutlery being moved around when there was nobody there. Apparently, a (deceased) resident always liked to move the chairs and cutlery around.

Val and Anne insisted they were not worried by the activity until an experiment seemed to take it to another level. One night when they were on together, they did an experiment to try and identify the apparitions. They wrote the question, 'Are you ex-residents here?' on a piece of paper together with a big 'YES' and 'NO'. They put a pen in the middle and left it in the Dining Room. Without anyone going near it the pen was pointing to the 'YES'. They were both convinced that this action had brought in a tall, dark figure. He was described as being at least six feet (2m) tall. Unlike the shadow ghosts he was dressed in a two-piece black suit and had black hair. He wasn't completely solid and according to those who witnessed him had no discernible face. The stuff of nightmares.

He frightened Val and Anne so much that they went to the local Spiritualist Church for help. Margaret was so concerned that she called in a Vicar to bless the building. Unfortunately this was of no help, so she then called in a clairvoyant. She identified the figure as 'Fred' and said he was no good in this world and no good in the world of spirit. The clairvoyant said, "tell it to go away, and be firm". Val followed the medium's advice and the next time she saw him told the figure to "pee off!" in no uncertain terms, and he apparently disappeared in a mist. By the time we visited he had not been seen since.

With all this alleged paranormal activity going on it might have been that some sort of mass hysteria was taking place within the home. If something really was going on here it would be reasonable to expect that Dennis and I would experience some of it too. We did.

In all, we conducted five investigations at the retirement home. It had been decided with Margaret that it would be best for just two of us to investigate between 10.00 pm and 5.00 am when the residents would be in their rooms. In the event, Dennis Bache and myself took on the case.

The initial investigation passed quietly at first. We set up thermometers by the door between the lounge and the dining room, on the table in the lounge and in the hall. We also installed a camcorder in the launderette facing the storeroom door and an audio recorder in the dining room by the lift. The only event of any note was a sudden 3^0C drop in temperature recorded on the thermometer in the doorway between the lounge and the dining room. The three-degree drop occurred around midnight. All of our subsequent temperature readings on this and other nights confirmed that the central heating was keeping the temperature in this area at a constant 21^0C. This was not necessarily significant apart from what happened in the exact same area later on. The following report was written immediately after the event by the author:

> The vigil with Dennis ended at approximately 5.00am. I collected the camcorder from the laundry and carried it along the connecting corridor to the dining room. As I passed the bedroom on the left a resident was complaining about her back. I was pre-occupied with thinking about the woman, deciding to tell Val and Anne about it, and at the same time negotiating the single step up to the dining room carrying the camera still attached to the extended tripod.
>
> As I looked up towards the dining room and the open door to the hall, I saw a solid looking figure wearing some sort of blue top disappear around the door on the right-hand side. I first assumed this was Dennis collecting the intercoms but soon realised that Dennis was winding cable in the dining room to my right. He had not seen anyone from where he was standing further down the dining room. I went immediately to the kitchen where Val and Anne were working. There was no sign of anyone in the hall, on the stairs or in the short corridor leading to the kitchen. Val and Anne had been in the kitchen for some minutes and were both dressed in white.
>
> Apart from the elderly residents, Dennis, the two care staff and myself were the only people in the building. If the figure had been a resident the person would still have been in the vicinity when I went

to look. Aside from this, the two carers always seemed to have an uncanny knack of knowing if someone was up and about, and they had not seen or heard anyone. Although I only saw the figure briefly, the sighting was long enough to discern what appeared to be a fairly young man wearing a blue top. He was moving quickly and gave the impression that he had just turned out of the dining room and into the hall, moving towards the kitchen. I only saw the rear half of the figure which was side on to me. There was no sound and I was not able to see a face due to the angle I was observing at. However, whilst the sighting was brief, the figure was directly in front of me at approximately six feet (2m) away. I estimated the time to be 5.13am. Unfortunately, the camcorder I was carrying was turned off at the time!

The camera and video setup used on the investigation

The care staff expressed no surprise at the sighting, except that most figures are seen as shadows whereas this was definitely solid-looking though very briefly observed.

Margaret was keen to know if we had experienced anything and met us at the start of our second investigation. Although this was not the phenomena we had been asked to investigate when reported back she immediately said, "Oh, I'm glad you've seen my son, he likes to come back to his old home". Unbeknownst to us, her son had been killed in a car accident when he was in his early twenties.

During our second investigation, the first event of the night occurred at approximately 11.15p m whilst the author was in the lounge:

> Val and Anne reported the floral perfume smell in the lounge. I went to the table where they were sitting but could smell nothing. I moved towards the mantelpiece by the clock and for a few seconds experienced a very strong smell of flowers or floral perfume. I could not identify the type of flowers. The smell lasted for about five seconds and then disappeared suddenly rather than fading away. No further trace of the smell could be found by any of us, and we discounted all the obvious sources of the smell such as automatic air fresheners as there weren't any. Val and Anne were amused at my suggestion it could have been the flowers in a vase on the mantelpiece. They were artificial!

By 11.30 pm we were sitting in the dining room. The following incident was described by Dennis:

> Andrew and myself were sat down in the lounge and the care staff were in the kitchen making coffee for us. We had been sat for about ten minutes when suddenly I saw a dark shadow pass along the wall behind Andrew. We had no idea what had caused the shadow and we tried to reproduce it for quite some time but without success.

Our third investigation was very quiet and found us wondering if the activity had subsided. However, out fourth investigation proved that it certainly had not.

We had two camcorders this time and decided to place them facing each other at either end of the dining room. This was the first time we had used camcorders in this way, but it is a technique we have made use of a number of times since.

Everything was quiet during the night, so at about 4.00 am we took a break in the conservatory at the front of the building. At 4.24 am we were talking about railways rather than ghosts when suddenly we both clearly heard a two-note whistle as though someone was trying to attract our attention. It seemed to come from the area of the front door or hall behind us. We both immediately investigated inside and outside the house but could find no possible source of the whistle. We had a good view outside and there was nobody in the driveway to the home or on the adjacent road. The two care staff on duty had heard us open the front door and came to the top of the stairs to see what we were doing. They had also heard the whistle and had assumed it was one of us. We all agreed it was a loud human-sounding whistle.

This was not the end of the incident, however, as we decided to replay the whistle on the recorder situated in the dining room closest to the conservatory. To our surprise, although our voices could be heard in the conservatory, the whistle had not been recorded. The tape was checked carefully to confirm the lack of any recorded whistle. The camcorder situated further down the lounge gave the same negative result. Subsequent tests to ascertain the source of the whistle were all clearly recorded on the equipment in the lounge.

The incident which occurred immediately afterwards is described by Dennis:

After thoroughly investigating the incident (whistle) it was time to change tapes. Andrew went to change the one in the launderette while I changed the dining room one. While doing so I went to the window and leant on the sill while waiting for Andrew to return. I was looking through the inside window and beyond the conservatory at 4.55 am. Suddenly I saw a male figure moving smartly and looking directly at me. For a second or so I thought it was someone outside but when it got to the reflection of the dining room wall it disappeared. At this point I realised that the figure itself was a reflection of a figure in the dining room behind me. The figure appeared to have a white face, with no discernible features and a grey top. No sound was heard. Although we had two camcorders in the dining room, one facing the window and one facing the lounge, we unfortunately did not capture the figure. We estimated that the figure had passed behind the one camcorder and the other one had just run to the end of the tape and Andrew had come to change it.

It is amazing how often something is seen just out of camera shot or when the recording is switched off. Unfortunately. we did not have the advantage of continuously recording headcams at that time. Quite why the whistle was clearly heard by everyone but not recorded was, and still is, a complete mystery that we have no explanation for.

Following this investigation, major alterations were made to the retirement home. The launderette area was extended, the kitchen was moved, and extra bedrooms added. According to Margaret, things had quietened down considerably while the alterations were being done, and we arranged to do a further investigation after the alterations were completed. According to the care staff present everything had been quiet and we agreed that the home looked and felt quite different from our previous visits. Nothing was experienced or recorded on this visit, and we agreed with the owner that she would contact us if things started up again. We had no further contact after this so can only assume that all was quiet from then on.

Changes to a property are often reputed to trigger paranormal activity. In this case however the opposite seems to have occurred in that major changes actually seemed to stop the activity. In reviewing this case, we realised that the alterations had been in the planning stages for a long time before any building work took place. Could it have been this that had started everything off in the first place? There certainly seems to have been such a correlation especially as everything settled down again once the building work was finished.

For the work done on the Hawthorn Retirement Home case, The Association for the Scientific Study of Anomalous Phenonema (ASSAP) awarded Dennis Bache and Andrew Homer the Michael Bentine Memorial Shield.

Holbeche House

The area around Holbeche House (also spelt Holbeach or Holbeache), right on the edge of the Black Country near Himley Hall, is steeped in history and saw violent events unfold which would echo down the years. The last action of the failed Gunpowder Plot of 1605 was played out in the November here and later, both King Charles I and King Charles II would pass through the region during the period of the English Civil War.

Holbeche House

After the Gunpowder Plot was discovered in London the remaining plotters made their way to the Midlands hoping for Catholic support. They stole fresh horses from Warwick Castle and replenished their stock of gunpowder from Hewell Grange, just outside Redditch. One of the plotters, Steven Littleton, owned Holbeche House and they thought would be a safe haven from pursuit by the High Sheriff of Worcestershire, Sir Richard Walsh, and his militia. It was not to be. During the journey to Holbeche House the gunpowder got damp whilst crossing a stream. On arrival, the powder was left to dry out in front of an open fire. As dangerous as this may seem, it was fairly common practice in those days. Unfortunately, a stray spark ignited the gunpowder injuring four of the men including their leader, Robert Catesby.

The remaining conspirators sat around this original fireplace

Two of the plotters, Stephen Lyttleton and Thomas Wintour went to 'Pepperhill' in Shropshire to request support from Sir John Talbot. He turned them away. Thomas Wintour returned to find Holbeche under siege by Sir Richard Walsh and 200 men. His brother, Robert Wintour, escaped the carnage and went on the run in the area with Stephen Lyttleton.

During the fierce battle, the plotters were either killed or captured and if anything, the plotters killed outright in the action at Holbeche were the fortunate ones as those captured would eventually be hung drawn and quartered. In a scene reminiscent of the film 'Butch Casidy and Sundance Kid' Robert Catesby and Thomas Percy resolved to die fighting. "Stand by me, Mr. Tom", said Catesby, "and we will die together". Making a last stand they were allegedly killed by a single musket shot fired by John Streete from Worcester who was rewarded for his marksmanship that day.

Robert Wintour and Stephen Lyttleton were apprehended two months later at Hagley Hall after being betrayed by the cook, John Fynwood. It is possibly the ghosts of these plotters who have been seen in the vicinity of Barnett Lane, Kingswinford. They were reputed to have hidden in the cellar of Paddock Cottage to escape the Sheriff of Worcester. There is a little row of shops there now, one of which used to be a hardware store. In May 2000, the author attended a paranormal investigation there after reports of poltergeist activity with things being moved around and sightings of a cavalier type apparition. Whilst no apparitions were seen, nevertheless a bunch of keys did start jangling for no apparent reason.

"The Gunpowder Plot: The conspirators' last stand at Holbeach House"
by Ernest Crofts

Another sighting on Barnett Lane involved three ladies who went to see why their security light had come on only to see a man they described as being in 17th century attire not walking, but gliding straight past the window. Then there was the couple who said, 'good evening' to a man dressed as a cavalier who they assumed was on his way to a fancy-dress party, only to watch him disappear straight through a thick hedge.

An apparition described as a cavalier has been seen on the other side of Holbeche House crossing the Himley Road oblivious to traffic. One credible witness to this was secretary, Diane Johnson, who was driving home one night. She told the author that in the headlights of her car she caught sight of a pair of knee-length cavalier type boots that passed quickly in front of her and into the grounds of Himley Hall. The park is now fenced off, but figures are seen crossing at the point where there used to be an old iron gate. Another apparition seen crossing here is that of a servant girl who also haunts the upper rooms of Himley Hall itself.

In the grounds of Himley Hall, we have yet another soldier described as English Civil War period who has been seen on occasions by night fishermen around the Great Lake. Charles I and his army camped for one night in the grounds of the old manor house where Himley Hall now stands, on the way to the ill-fated battle of Naseby. Richard Symonds accompanied the Royalist army and wrote in his diary for the 16th of May 1645 that, 'one soldjer was hanged for mutiny' trying to desert whilst they were camped at Himley. Justice was swift in those days.

The siege of Holbeche House has given rise to the now famous ghost story of Gideon Grove but all may not be quite as it seems. According to the story, Gideon Grove was a young groom at Holbeche and played no part in either the plot or the siege. During the attack he fled in fear and tried to make his way back home to Trysull. He was running through marshy land along where the Bridgnorth Road is now. Unfortunately, he was spotted by some of the sheriff's men and pursued on horseback. The helpless Gideon stood no chance and was quickly apprehended. Rather than taking him prisoner, the sheriff's men used their pikes to push Gideon into the marsh and held him under until he drowned.

This led to stories of phantom horseman along the Bridgnorth Road at Wombourne particularly in the mid-1960s. The story of Gideon Grove first surfaces in the Black Country Bugle. Allegedly, the story was taken from a book of poems by the 19th century Rhymer Greensill. What better name than Rhymer for a poet? No evidence of this book has been found beyond the copy owned by Harry Taylor, the founder and editor of the Bugle. Harry Taylor wrote stories under a number of pseudonyms including Aristotle Tump and others.

An ex-police officer, John Mellor, claimed to know the identities of three 'phantom' horsemen who would ride hell for leather at night through Wombourne. He claimed they were a local Doctor, farmer, and a businessman's daughter. Yet another rider dressed all in black would 'borrow' horses and ride at night sometimes putting them back in the wrong fields! Mellor claimed to have had a quiet word with all concerned and put a stop to it. However, it still didn't stop people having odd experiences along the Bridgnorth Road at night. Both Joe Green in 1971 and Monica Bowen in 1973 experienced having their vehicles cut out and horsemen pass close by. Joe Green also claimed to have seen a horseman clutching his neck as though wounded. On both occasions the vehicles came to life again once the horsemen had passed. Even though the 1960's riders were identified by Mellor, we cannot know exactly what it was that Joe Green and Monica Bowen experienced.

The priest hole with a glass viewing window

By the time our group was invited to investigate Holbeche House it had become a well-established care home. Both staff and residents had been reporting shadowy figures, the ghost of a gentleman in a tall hat and a cavalier seen in the lounge. Staff had been kicked or pushed on the grand staircase and the night before our visit the period wooden front door, which was always secured to keep residents safe, had opened all by itself. All of this activity was taking place in the older part of the building at the front which still bears the scars of musket shot from the 1605 siege. Being a Catholic house, it was no surprise to see a priest hole for hiding Catholic clergy which had been made into a feature by placing a thick glass viewing window over it. We were told that shadows and dark shapes had been seen particularly in the entrance hall and around the magnificent staircase. A wireless video camera was set up here to hopefully record any activity. The investigation started quietly but in the early hours of the morning things started to happen.

Firstly, in a room off the entrance hall a shadow was seen moving across one of the walls.

Throughout any of our investigations, vigil sheets were always filled in to accurately record the timings of any phenomena or indeed anything such as someone moving a chair or taking a flash photograph that other investigators may see or hear. In this way, at the end of an investigation the sheets can be compared in order to eliminate anything that could be put down to natural causes. As an example, somebody moving their chair on wooden floorboards can echo right through a quiet building.

Shortly after the shadow was seen in the side room the group in the entrance witnessed a dark shadowy figure move across under the staircase and disappear into the wall towards the priest hole on the other side. Obviously, the time of this was recorded and as luck would have it the video camera was recording and pointing in the right direction to record it. At the same time Julie Hunt by the priest hole saw a dark shadow emerge from the same wall before disappearing. Again, the exact time was noted, and the vigil sheets would later confirm that this was the same shadowy figure seen on both sides of the wall in the entrance hall.

At the end of the investigation, everyone was naturally keen to see the recording made of the dark figure in the entrance hall. The camera was wirelessly operated and so was not directly connected to the recorder. During the period of interest all that was recorded was static. The camera and recorder were carefully checked later and found to be working perfectly. Very disappointing, but it is amazing just how many times over the years equipment has failed for whatever reason just at the crucial moment.

Katie's Café

Throughout all of our investigations over many years it was very rare to encounter anything that could be described as downright unpleasant. Katie's Café in Wellington, Shropshire was the exception. The café itself was very pleasant and popular with locals and shoppers. It was quite a long building with a main entrance off the road to the front, and a service entrance at the back where the kitchen was. Halfway down the seating area was a door. The café was bright and cheerful in stark contrast to what lay behind the door. Customers had no access of course, and probably would not have given it a second thought.

Immediately behind this plain, wooden door was a very steep staircase. The whole area was dingy and dark. The floors above were unfurnished and clearly had not been used for decades. Café staff did not like even going up there, but the empty rooms provided useful storage for non-food items. The top floor had a landing with rooms to the left and right. Unlike the cheery café, these rooms were dark and dusty with covered windows and the occasional stick of furniture left over from when they were once rented out.

The top floor landing

We never did discover exactly how old the building was, but in the 19th century Wellington was developing into a modern town and many low roofed timber framed buildings were clad with bricks and new storeys added or else replaced entirely by brick.

Our group was called in to investigate when the café owner and her staff started having unnerving experiences in the building, particularly upstairs on the top floor. The owner had heard whispering in the kitchen area when there had been nobody else there. She had also seen the figure of an old lady in the same area. She was recognised as the mother of the two sisters who used to own the café. However, it was upstairs and particularly the room on the right hand side of the top floor landing that was really causing concern. The room had been divided at some point in time to create a bathroom, but other than that was empty.

Nobody liked going up there as they were convinced there was something very unpleasant in that room, although nothing had actually been seen. One of the waitresses had suffered a severe panic attack on the landing caused by an overwhelming feeling of sheer terror. She now refused to go up there at all on her own. Staff members had also heard their names being called in the room above the kitchen. Even when there was nobody up there, footsteps were often to be heard going up and down the wooden stairs.

We were able to mount a number of investigations at the café involving different members of the team. Because we had one particular room that was causing unpleasant reactions in people, we decided to conduct a simple experiment. We made sure that only people who had previously been to the café knew which room was involved. When someone new came with us, they would be taken around the rooms upstairs and asked to note down what they felt. The results were very interesting. Almost without exception, the upstairs room with the bathroom was picked out as having a bad atmosphere, feeling very unpleasant, unwelcoming, or just downright scary.

On our first investigation at the café the author was setting up some newly purchased low light video equipment on the top floor landing (see also Would you believe it?):

I was setting up some video equipment to monitor the doorway into the room with the walled off bathroom. All was going well but a little slowly as the equipment was new and this was the first time it had been used on a live investigation. Having had help to carry the gear upstairs, everyone else had gone back down to the café leaving me on my own. Whilst concentrating on setting up the equipment I suddenly began to feel very uneasy. The feeling got worse, and I had the overwhelming impression that a black shape, something very dark, was filling the doorway in front of me although I couldn't actually see anything. Perhaps foolishly in retrospect, I stood my ground and didn't move. After what was probably just a few seconds but seemed longer whatever it was went back into the room, and the feeling of uneasiness lifted. No wonder that poor waitress had a panic attack.

The author was not the only investigator to feel there was something very dark in that same room as others experienced it as well on subsequent investigations. On one occasion the door to the café opened and closed loudly on its own. At the end of that investigation at about 3.00 am everyone when was downstairs in the café, loud footsteps were heard on the stairs behind the closed door. An immediate check confirmed there was nobody left upstairs.

The creepy room with the walled off bathroom

On our final investigation at the café, the author and a colleague were doing a 45-minute vigil session on the top floor:

> The room on the left-hand side of the landing was accessed via a short corridor. As with the other rooms it was dark due to the windows being boarded. Whilst my colleague was in the room behind me, I had decided to place a chair in the small connecting corridor looking towards the room with the bathroom. It was 1.45 am and I remember turning around to look behind me after hearing a noise. My colleague signalled to say it was it was him. I turned back and there was a figure standing in the doorway across the landing. It appeared to be a man, and he was standing with his back against the door frame. I could only see him in silhouette so could not make out any detail except that he was quite tall and of medium build. He was also wearing what appeared to be a top hat. Just as I was about to alert my colleague he disappeared.

Because of the footsteps heard on the stairs at the end of the previous investigation, and the door to the café opening, the low light video camera was covering that area and not the landing. Unfortunately, due to a change of circumstances with the business, this would prove to be the last time we were able to conduct any research at Katie's Café and so we were unable to take this active investigation any further.

Lake Vyrnwy

Whilst writing *Haunted Hostelries of Shropshire* (Amberley, 2012) a rather poignant ghost story came to light with a connection to Lake Vyrnwy in Wales. It required a drive out to The Green Inn, Llangedwyn, situated in the beautiful Tanat Valley. Despite the Welsh sounding name, it falls just within Shropshire.

The Green Inn Llangedwyn

During the building of the Lake Vyrnwy reservoir and the dam in the 1880s something like a thousand workmen were living in the area during the eight-year construction project for Liverpool Corporation. The desperate need to provide clean water for grossly overcrowded cities during the Industrial Revolution led to ambitious schemes such as the Vyrnwy Waterworks Project serving Liverpool and Merseyside. Many men understandably wanted their families nearby and moved them into the area during the lengthy construction period.

A 'lost' village lies beneath the flooded valley of the River Vyrnwy. When conditions are just right the eerie ruins of the original Llanwddyn can be glimpsed beneath the waters of the reservoir. The whole village including the church was relocated further up the valley before it was flooded. Even corpses were exhumed and reinterred in the new village churchyard.

According to local legend, the lake was used for practice bombing runs in preparation for Operation Chastise during World War Two. Now famous as the 'Dambusters' raid, the German Möhne and Eder dams were breached and the Sorpe dam damaged in May 1943 by Lancasters of 617 Squadron. This mistaken belief seems to have originated because at least one scene in the classic 1955 movie, The Dambusters, was filmed at Lake Vyrnwy.

In the 1880s, the landlord of The Green Inn was renting his upstairs rooms to the families of workmen employed on the dam. One such family had a little girl who always liked to sit in one of the upstairs windows waiting for her father to come down the road from Lake Vyrnwy. One fateful day he was killed in a dreadful accident at the dam. His name was inscribed along with other poor souls on a memorial obelisk overlooking Lake Vyrnwy. Health and safety left much to be desired in Victorian engineering and such tragic accidents were all too common. To this day, visitors entering this quaint country pub for the first time have been known to enquire who the pretty little girl is, sitting in the upstairs window of what is now the restaurant and staring out along the road in the direction of Lake Vyrnwy.

On completion of the dam the obelisk was erected by the workmen themselves as a memorial to the forty-four men who died during the construction project. Of these, ten men are listed as being killed on site. Given the awful working conditions and scant medical care at the time it is highly likely that those not killed outright in accidents died later of injury or disease.

Having obtained the story from The Green Inn and learning about the memorial obelisk it just had to be visited. Unfortunately, the deadline for the book meant that publication took place before it was possible to visit the area again.

In the event it was some time after publication that a friend and I decided to explore the Welsh Highland Railway. On the return journey from Wales, we took a slight detour to enable me to finally visit the memorial obelisk. It was not easy to find. On the approach to the dam a large memorial built by Liverpool Corporation commemorates the dignitaries who were responsible for commissioning the Vyrnwy Waterworks Project, but not the men who lost their lives.

The Lake Vyrnwy Memorial Obelisk

A drive along both sides of the dam gave no clue as to where the obelisk might be. Eventually, we stopped to enquire at a local shop and the local lady in there seemed quite surprised that I even knew about the obelisk. She also wanted to know why I was trying to find it! Explanation given, the directions she gave took us to a local hotel, The Lake Vyrnwy, with instructions to follow a path leading off the car park. Finding the path at all required further assistance from a helpful gentleman doing some work on the outside of the hotel. By this time, it was getting late on a wet, dull afternoon. My friend opted to stay in the car rather than venture up the tree covered hillside. Judging by the overgrown state of the path, and the absence of any signs pointing the way, it was obvious that few people ever visited this sadly forgotten memorial. The path eventually petered out altogether and I was on the verge of giving up and going back down to the car when suddenly the memorial became visible through the trees. The sheer size of the obelisk came as quite a surprise when I finally reached it.

The names of the forty-four workers who died are recorded around the square base of the obelisk which, to give some idea of the scale, is itself over six feet tall. The names of the ten men who were killed on site are inscribed on the side of the obelisk directly facing the lake and dam which claimed their lives.

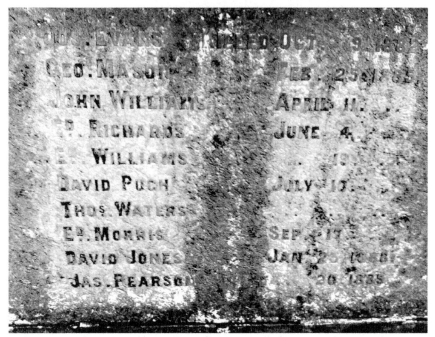

The names of the ten men who died

As I stood there reading the names of these ten men and wondering who the father of the little girl might be, I heard my friend making her way along the path. She came up and stood right behind me. As I turned to speak to her, I realised there was nobody there. The path and the woods were deserted. Walking back down I felt a strange sense of closure, as though I had opened a door to a tragic event in the past by publishing the story of the girl in the window, but then closed it again by paying my respects at the obelisk. On reaching the car I asked my friend if she had decided to get out and walk up the path after all. She hadn't.

Legend of Alton Towers

Alton Towers is well known as a theme park, but it was once owned by the Earl's of Shrewsbury. The once magnificent gothic revival house is mainly in ruins but parts of it have been incorporated into the theme park's attractions. Redeveloped from a former hunting lodge in the 19th century by Charles Talbot, 15th Earl of Shrewsbury, he unwittingly created the legend of the 'Chained Oak' which inspired the present-day ride, Hex - The Legend of the Towers. Unusually this is situated in part of the Grade II listed building.

The mainly ruined Alton Towers house

There are variations on the legend, but the central theme is that the Earl, returning home one night, was forced to halt his coach for an old woman standing in the road. She begged to be given a coin, but the Earl was not one to part with his money so easily and he rudely refused. The old woman cursed him saying that each time a branch would fall from a nearby oak tree a member of his family would die. One version of the story has a member of the household dying that very night during a violent storm, whilst another has it that the Earl's son was killed in a riding accident near the oak tree the following day. Either way the Earl had the oak tree chained up to prevent any further deaths. A fanciful legend perhaps, except that the 'Chained Oak' still exists outside the grounds of Alton Towers to this day and can be visited although perhaps best avoided if your name happens to be Talbot!

The Chained Oak (Gary Rogers, CC BY-SA 2.0)

Right from when Hex first opened there were reports of strange things happening that were not part of the ride. Small pebbles would be thrown at people in the queue, and ghostly children in Victorian or Edwardian style clothing seen on occasions. Poltergeist activity has been experienced around the ruins and in particular, doors opening and closing for no apparent reason as if someone were passing through. It might be the lady in a long dress who has also been seen striding purposefully through the ruined building. Add to this, sightings of the old lady who cursed the earl, ghostly soldiers, and a large black dog it is easy to see why Alton Towers has acquired quite a reputation for being haunted.

We were very fortunate in having the opportunity to mount an overnight investigation at Alton Towers. Although we found the area containing Hex was interesting and not surprisingly atmospheric, it was not at all active on the night our group investigated. An interesting incident did occur though outside in front of the ruined house. We had been told where we could go around the building so as not to attract the attention of the security guards who we could see patrolling the park throughout the night. It was dark but there were enough external lights to see by. We were heading towards our next vigil location and the author happened to look back:

> We were the only team meant to be outside in this particular location. Having got the feeling that someone was behind us, I turned around just in time to see what appeared to be an adult with a child. They had come from the direction of the main park where there should not have been anyone and went down towards the Great Hall that we had just come from. Obviously, there were no children on site. They were only briefly visible in the pool of light coming from one of the exterior wall lamps. I immediately went back to see who they were and retraced our steps back towards the hall. They could only have followed the same route we had taken through a long a high-walled passageway. There was nobody in sight, and they would not have had enough time to walk the entire length of the passageway to the only unlocked door right at the other end.

Ghostly children are associated with the nearby Hex ride, but this certainly appeared to be an adult with a child, although it was not possible to discern any detail such as clothing apart from their relative heights. Whilst doing some research for a later article the author discovered that shadowy figures had been reported fairly regularly in this same area. One such sighting was by a member of staff who had been on his own in the Chapel lighting candles for an evening event. He heard footsteps but didn't see anyone until he had finished and was outside the building on his way to the next job. He was taken by surprise when a shadowy figure suddenly passed by close to his left and promptly disappeared.

We found the extensive block which had once contained the kitchens to be quite atmospheric. There was much low-level poltergeist activity reported here, particularly with doors opening and closing. Towards the end of our vigil in the kitchen area, this door movement was caught almost accidentally on the author's headcam.

Outside the substantial wooden rear doors to the kitchen area there was a sheltered area bounded by a perimeter wall with a narrow brick tunnel leading to another part of the park. I had just walked through the tunnel simply out of curiosity and was on my way back through it. A fellow investigator was waiting for me outside the kitchen door. I knew that both halves of the rear door had been fully open but noticed on my way back that one half was now closed. However, as I moved towards it the door slowly opened again. The headcam was running so a quick check of the footage on the LCD monitor showed that it had been recorded.

The door opens quite slowly as I approached the end of the tunnel. There were other investigators in the corridor behind the door, but they were much further up. Having realised that the door had closed and then opened again for no apparent reason, we tried to replicate it. The door was quite heavy, and it could not be made to both open and close under its own volition. The door can be seen on the video recording to be opening quite slowly and deliberately. 🎥 1

The headcam footage before entering the tunnel clearly shows the door fully open. During the short time the author was in the tunnel, the door had closed and then opened again as caught on the headcam. There was nobody else present apart from a fellow investigator who had not moved from the little yard at the rear of the kitchen but had not noticed the rear door opening and closing.

🎥 1

Littledean Jail

Littledean Jail at Littledean near Cinderford in the Royal Forest of Dean is definitely not for the faint hearted. Even though it is now a museum, potential visitors are given a stark warning before entering the former 18th century prison:

From serial killers to satanism and capital punishment to the paranormal, Littledean Jail is packed to the rafters with a diverse collection of the most bizarre and some downright macabre exhibits. Littledean Jail also has a reputation for being very haunted.

Inside one of the many museum galleries

Completed in 1791, Littledean House of Correction as it was known was based on ideas stemming from the ground-breaking 1779 Penitentiary Act. All but the most dangerous prisoners would be confined to, 'solitary imprisonment accompanied by well-regulated labour and religious instruction'. These notions of prison reform were championed by Gloucestershire gentleman and magistrate Sir George Onesiphorus Paul. He employed the services of noted prison architect, William Blackburn, to design the building. Blackburn was not to see it completed though, as he died in 1790. It was his brother-in-law William Hobson who would see the project through to completion in 1791. As constructed, the building had two storeys with a central block for offices and staff accommodation together with two wings for the prisoners. It was enlarged in 1844 and a third story added to the central block. An outer wall with gatehouse surrounded the building and its four courtyards.

Littledean Jail

As a House of Correction, also known as a Brideswell, it was never the intention to house long term prisoners. Rather, implementing the progressive ideas of Sir George Onesiphorus Paul, short term prisoners were housed in reasonable accommodation and engaged in productive employment. Even so, at this period in time men, women and children would be incarcerated together. Children could be felons in their own right or else born in jail to imprisoned mothers. This may well explain the ghostly cries and screams of young children heard echoing through the building. People could be imprisoned for what would be regarded as trivial reasons these days. The first prisoner to be admitted to Littledean was Joseph Marshall on the 18th of November 1781. His crime? Stealing a spade.

Littledean jail may have been established with good intentions, but it did not remain that way. Even so, it was a major influence on the design of London's Pentonville Prison. It was reported in 1830 that a hand-crank mill had been installed for prisoners sentenced to hard labour. It was used for grinding corn and prisoners could work up to nine hours in the summer and five hours in the winter. The work was hard and soul destroying but it got worse. Gloucestershire Archives have a record of plans for a shed to enclose a treadmill in 1842. This was a large cylinder with steps and individual bays. This forced prisoners to keep walking on the spot for hours at a time. Described as 'cruel and barbaric' the use of treadmills was finally abolished in 1902 following the 1898 Prison Act.

The treadmill at Pentoville Prison in 1895 which was modelled on Lttledean

Littledean ceased to be a House of Correction in 1854 becoming instead a police station and remand prison. From 1874 one wing was used as a petty sessional court. It was here that the last witchcraft trial in Gloucestershire was held in May 1906. Ellen Hayward, known locally as 'Old Ellen' of Cinderford was a 'wise woman' and herbalist. In 1905 reports of witchcraft and the casting of spells on members of the Markey family even reached Parliament. Ellen was accused of bewitching one James Davis, a local farmer, and causing him to fall ill. Ellen denied casting any such spells and the magistrate's agreed as they dismissed the case. Appropriate perhaps then that Littledean now houses exhibits connected with witchcraft.

The police station closed in 1972 and from 1985 the building was used as records storage and computer centre. It is now a privately owned museum. If buildings can hold strong emotions, Littledean Jail has certainly experienced more than its fair share.

Hardly surprising then that Littledean Jail has a frightening reputation for being haunted, and by more than one entity. Most disturbing is the presence of children in the prison. They are often heard running unseen around the building. Reputedly, in the 1830s at least three unmarried mothers gave birth whilst incarcerated here and may account for the unmistakeable cry of a newborn baby heard around the area of the cells. If the reports are accurate one of the babies born here sadly did not survive being locked up with the mother. The paranormal activity here is not just limited to overnight ghost hunts. At any time of the day or night loud footsteps can be heard echoing through the corridors and heavy cell doors being banged shut when there is nobody there. Other unexplained noises are also regularly heard.

The activity is not just auditory either. Dark figures have been seen moving about and seemingly watching from the shadows. Some visitors and ghost hunters claim to have been unfortunate enough to experience a malevolent spirit who tries to shove people out of his way. He is said to be the ghost of a particularly cruel jailer who had a singular dislike for the children and would pass from cell to cell terrorising the helpless prisoners supposedly in his care.

An opportunity to investigate Littledean Jail came about through our contacts with a local Gloucestershire group. Apart from the presence of one of the owners, our joint group would have sole access to the prison. Despite being such an intriguing building to be in, the investigation was fairly quiet up until the final session. We had split into small groups of investigators, and all agreed on 45-minute 'vigil' sessions which would ensure everyone was quiet during these times. We moved around after each session to experience as much of the building as possible. Towards the end of the investigation there was some discussion as to whether we should pack up and go as it had been so quiet or have just one more vigil. The majority voted for one last vigil session.

As we had come a fair distance for this we voted to spend as much time as possible and continue the investigation with a final session. I'm glad we did. For the last session, our little group opted to go up to the cells on the narrow second floor landing. Here we split. Three of our group positioned themselves at the end of the landing whilst Steve Willis and myself decided to sit in one of the cells with the heavy iron door closed. Things started quietly enough, but in the cell we began to hear what sounded like something heavy being dragged along the floor outside in the corridor. It was the sort of noise which would be made if dragging something like a large sack of flour, certainly not metallic or furniture sounding.

We resisted the temptation to open the cell door until the sound had ceased as we knew the other half of our group must have been experiencing it as well. It turned out that the others, positioned just a short distance away along the landing had been sitting quietly the whole time but had heard and seen nothing. From our point of view from inside the cell the dragging sound was definitely in the corridor immediately outside even though the people stationed there were completely unaware of it.

The final debrief revealed that our dragging sound had been the high point of our investigation there. It was a bit of a shame that this only occurred at the end of our time at Littledean Jail leaving us no opportunity for any further investigation of the landing and prison cells.

Mason's Ironstone Pottery

It was July 1998, and an urgent invitation came from a paranormal group based in North Staffordshire. Through someone who used to work there, they had been granted access to the disused Mason's Ironstone Pottery in Broad Street, Stoke on Trent. The urgency was because the building was due to be demolished and cleared for redevelopment. A Tesco Supermarket now stands on the site. In fact, the bulldozers moved in on the Monday following our investigation on the previous Saturday into Sunday morning. This was to be the first and last time a paranormal investigation would take place in the historic pottery.

Mason's Ironstone Pottery Stoke on Trent

Stoke on Trent is known for pottery of course and the Mason's Ironstone site had been in continuous production for over 250 years being established in the early 1700s. The pottery had been substantially rebuilt in 1815 following a rectangular courtyard design, common at that time. In 1813, Charles Mason had registered his 'Patent Ironstone China' which proved immensely popular. By 1848 though his fortunes had changed, and he went bankrupt. It was Francis Morley who purchased Charles Mason's moulds and began production of the famous 'Mason's Ironstone Pottery' at the Hanbury site factory. The factory was eventually owned by Wedgewood and continued production right up until 1998 when it was finally closed.

In the event, Gareth, Ron, and the author from Parasearch joined Dave, Pauline, Matt, and Joanne from the North Staff's group to conduct the overnight investigation from Saturday until Sunday morning. It was Pauline who was able to supply information about the paranormal activity here, as she had worked at Masons before it shut down. On one occasion, she had seen the ghost of a deceased colleague, Lee Vie, standing in the area known to staff as 'kiln square'. He was wearing his protective leather overalls as he would have done for work.

Poltergeist type activity had apparently been regularly experienced around the area containing the long, narrow Gilding Shop and the adjacent Colour Room. In the latter, things had often been inexplicably knocked off shelves. It was the Gilding Shop though that had been subject to the most frequent activity. Right down the shop were positioned the 'gold bins'. These were presumably used to collect all the excess gold when gilding the pottery. At times, and usually early in the morning, the bins would be knocked loudly in turn from the bottom of the shop to the top. It would sound as though someone was thumping them with their fist as they walked past, even though there was nobody there.

The Gilding Shop with video recorder on the right

On the night of the investigation, we all met up outside. The North Staff's group had been given the keys to the building and trusted to lock it up again after our investigation. For security reasons, we locked the doors again once we were inside to avoid the possibility of any unwanted visitors. For the most part, the whole factory was in complete darkness. The electricity supply had been disconnected in readiness for demolition, all except one small office with had a light and a mains socket. This turned out to be some way from the areas of interest and so there was no possibility of running power cables for the low light video cameras. We were to rely on battery power and torchlight for this investigation.

We split into pairs and agreed a rotation of areas to investigate. From 11.15 pm until midnight, Matt from the North Staff's group and the author were stationed in the Gilding Shop. We had with us a tripod mounted low light video camera running off a 12-volt camping battery. The camera had infrared lights but otherwise the shop was in total darkness. We were sitting looking down the shop although we could not see anything without switching on a torch.

The fire door leading to another part of the factory

Behind us a few metres away was a fire door which was locked surprisingly, although we had easy access to the area behind the door. This was not a direct exit but led to a much lower part of the pottery down a flight of metal stairs. We were a long way from any external doors.

It was exactly 11.42 pm when the door behind us suddenly started banging and the doorknob rattling as though someone was desperate to get through. Torches on, we got to the door as quickly as possible, but even so the banging had stopped. We fully expected the rest of our small team to appear and see what all the noise was about, but surprisingly nobody did, not even the couple in the nearby Colour Room. It had certainly been loud enough to echo around the empty factory, but somehow seemed to have been confined to just the Gilding Shop.

Having realised there was nobody there, we quickly checked the other side of the door. Not only was there no one in the lower part of the pottery but we realised there had been no sound of footsteps on the metal stairs either going up or down.

It turned out that none of our team had heard anything apart from Matt and myself, although all members were accounted for at the time. This was very hard to believe given how loud the banging had been. The video camera though had been running, although we were not sure whether it would have picked up the sound of the door as it was quite a distance away and the microphone was pointed in the opposite direction down the Gilding Shop. Fortunately, the noise from the door had been recorded and the other team members were amazed when it was played back that they had not heard it themselves. 🎥 1 We never did work out why no one else heard it when it was picked up so clearly on the Gilding Shop camera.

The rest of the night was quiet with no repetition of the door banging. It was a great shame that there was no further opportunity to return to Mason's Ironstone Pottery but at least we had got to investigate it just the once.

It is interesting to speculate who or what might have come through the fire door in the Gilding Shop that night if had it not been locked.

🎥 1

Red Lion and Avebury

Avebury Village is partly enclosed by Avebury Henge and Stone Circles. Built during the Neolithic period it includes the largest stone circle ever to be built in Britain. The Red Lion sits right within the stones and has an enviable reputation for being haunted.

The Red Lion within Avebury Henge and Stone Circles (Nessy-Pic, CC BY-SA 3.0)

Part of the pub has been built over an ancient well which is now glass topped and a popular feature with visitors. The best-known ghost at the Red Lion is Florrie. During the English Civil War, Florrie's husband went off to fight and while he was away, she took a lover. The husband returned unexpectedly to find his wife with another. In a fit of jealous rage, he killed the lover and then turned his attentions to Florrie. Having slit her throat, he threw her lifeless body down the well which is now such a focal point in the bar. Her ghost has allegedly been seen emerging from the well. She seems to be particularly drawn to bearded men and will sometimes make her presence felt by swinging the heavy wood and metal chandelier in the restaurant. Whether she is looking for revenge on her murderous husband or searching for her former lover is open to speculation. They would both have likely had beards in the 17th century though.

Ancient well now a focal point in the pub bar (Andy Dolman, CC BY-SA 2.0)

Other ghosts reported at the Red Lion include two children and a lady who sits and writes. They are mostly seen around the bedrooms. A farmer, double crossed and murdered by fugitives he was trying to hide, is also said to haunt his former home. In common with many other places, dark shadowy figures have been reported in different parts of the building. Another story which is perhaps more legend than actual apparition concerns the courtyard. If a phantom coach pulled by phantom horses draws up it is a sure harbinger of death or disaster for someone at the pub.

The author was fortunate in being invited to investigate the Red Lion, and stay over in one of the guest rooms, given the distance from the Black Country. Despite the covered well situated in the bar, much of the activity seemed to centre around the larger restaurant. This is where the heavy wood and metal chandelier hangs, favoured by the ghost of Florrie. During another investigation here, Mark and Julie Hunt saw the chandelier start swinging for no apparent reason around 4.00 am. It swung for around 20 minutes before stopping. Interesting to note that Mark had a beard!

It was a quiet night as investigations go apart from a couple of odd occurrences in the restaurant (see also Would you Believe it?). A window looking out onto the car park started to vibrate for no apparent reason. On checking outside there was no noticeable wind although the window had been vibrating quite violently for some seconds. It is worth noting that my colleague, Mark, and the author were both sporting healthy beards at the time!

Later on in the investigation, there were a number of sightings from different team members of the shadowy figures in the bar area. A door near the well seemed particularly prone to this as two investigators and the author saw a dark shadow move across it. In all cases, following careful checking, there was no logical explanation for the moving shadows to have been there.

If anything, the most interesting event occurred at dawn as we were staying over. A couple of us went out to look at the stones while it was quiet and with nobody else about:

I had been reading about some research done by Paul Devereaux concerning standing stones and ultrasound. Ultrasound is high frequency sound well above the range of human hearing. Bats are well known natural sources of infrasound for echolocation. I had a tuneable ultrasound device with me, commonly known as a 'bat detector' although unfortunately it had no option for recording. We wandered around the stones for a while, enjoying the peace and quiet of the early morning, and not really expecting to pick anything up. We had made our way over to a line of fairly large stones by the National Trust Museum. Surprisingly, next to one of these stones we picked up some ultrasound. It was very high frequency being near the maximum for the device of 150 kHz and very quiet, but it was there. We found that we could map out the sound around the stone and it spread out for roughly 1.5 metres in all directions. Unfortunately, we could not pinpoint the source except it was definitely coming from the stone. We tested adjacent stones and heard nothing. Just as we were working out how to try and record it the sound disappeared.

Although we tried again before leaving Avebury, there was no sign of the elusive ultrasound. The sound we picked up was steady and constant before it disappeared and nothing like the ultrasound generated by bats or insects.

Smethwick Swimming Centre

S methwick Swimming Centre is also known as Smethwick Baths and Thimblemill Baths. It is a superb Art Deco Moderne Style Grade II listed building opened in 1933. Originally, the swimming pool was only used during the summer. In the winter it was boarded over and used for dances, concerts, and shows. During World War Two, the building played an important part in the war effort. The local Civil Defence Service used it as a base and the maze of service tunnels and rooms below the building served as a community air raid shelter. During this time part of the building was used as a morgue for victims of the bombing raids. Right next to the baths was an American supply base, and Italian prisoners of war were billeted nearby.

Smethwick Swimming Centre

There is a long and varied history of hauntings here. Even as early as the late 1930s, there were reports of the ghosts of three children and in particular a little girl in the building. By all accounts they are still here, as staff regularly hear them laughing often when the building is empty and being locked up at night. Staff often know when they are present because the air will become chilled but returns to normal as soon as someone says 'hello' to them. There is an amazing network of service tunnels and rooms beneath the public areas known as the subway. It is here that a man in a green uniform is regularly seen. Sightings of him usually precede the plant machinery breaking down and it is thought that he was once a maintenance engineer.

Some of the apparitions seen in the subway are clearly connected with wartime activity. A figure described as a 'spiv', someone who used to trade in illegal black market goods, has been seen as has a uniformed American airman. A German airman in full flying gear has also been seen near an old escape tunnel. As to why these figures should be here, it is said that the Americans would bring any downed German airmen into the tunnels for interrogation. It is possible, as Americans were stationed next door in the supply depot.

The Second World War air raid shelter

Our first investigation of this fascinating site took place on the 13th of February 2009. As usual the team split into small groups to investigate the different areas on a rotational basis. The investigation passed off fairly quietly except at 12.15 am outside the old air raid shelter investigator Steve Potter reported that:

On a walk around the basement area with Frank Smith and while taking readings, I turned into one corridor and observed a figure at the far end of the corridor; the figure walked left to right across the corridor.

The figure was male five feet seven inches tall approximately, he was strawberry blonde or redheaded wearing green or grey clothing. Interestingly the figure appeared to be heading towards the Second World War shelter.

This matches perfectly reports of the 'maintenance engineer' figure that had been frequently reported in the subway. We had a video camera running in the air raid shelter and, at first, we thought we had recorded the phantom figure. However, a later close examination showed that we could not be certain whether it was the figure or one of our own investigators who walked past the partly open door. Our low light cameras at the time were black and white. Otherwise, the colour of the clothing the figure was wearing might have confirmed whether or not we had indeed captured the apparition of the maintenance man.

One of the main subway corridors

One aspect of the subway, given the presence of machinery and tunnels, was the possibility of infrasound being present. That is, low frequency sound below the threshold of human hearing which is normally 20 Hz to 20 kHz. Below 20 Hz is infrasound. We were fortunate to have been involved in ground-breaking work by the late Vic Tandy of Coventry University. He became interested in infrasound and its possible effects after experiencing a seemingly paranormal event in his supposedly haunted laboratory at Warwick. He suddenly felt anxious as though someone was watching him and saw a grey blob out of the corner of his eye. When he tried to look at it directly, it had disappeared. The following day he happened to be working on one of his fencing foils and had the handle held in a vice. The blade started vibrating for no apparent reason. Vic reasoned that the only possible source of the vibration was an extraction fan. He had equipment to measure the frequency of vibration from the fan and it was 18.98 Hz. This is virtually the frequency at which the human eye resonates at 19 Hz. He further concluded that this could have been the cause of him seeing the dark figure. The size of the room caused a standing wave which was causing the fencing foil to vibrate.

Parasearch members including the author were pleased to meet with Vic and receive a detailed explanation of his theories. We were also treated to a visit to the allegedly haunted cellar where he had conducted his initial experiments in order to produce a ground-breaking paper, *The Ghost in the Machine*. Working on a design produced by Vic Tandy, electronic's expert Frank Smith was able to construct a viable infrasound meter for use on our investigations.

Before our next investigation at the Swimming Centre, a great deal of work was done by George Gregg, Frank Smith, Steve Potter, and the author to construct a large-scale experiment to test whether infrasound in the subway tunnels could possibly be causing seemingly paranormal effects. The experiment was designed to see if there was any significant difference in the perceptions of investigators between areas of infrasound and non-infrasound.

Six areas of high and low infrasound were identified by Frank Smith and Steve Potter. They were the only members of the team who knew which was which during the experiment. The rest of the team were divided up into three groups and rotated around the designated areas. Every five minutes each team member noted down on a record sheet any experiences involving the five senses of sight, hearing, touch, smell, and taste together with any emotional responses felt.

During the experiment which lasted until 2.00 am one member of the team felt the presence of a small, playful child by the door to the air raid shelter. Another member of the team felt something cold touch their arm which is also associated with the presence of the children. Perhaps they were curious as to what we were doing!

When the results of the experiment were analysed, it was found that there was no significant difference as far as experiences were concerned between the areas of infrasound and non-infrasound. This experiment could not therefore confirm any correlation between infrasound and paranormal experiences in the tunnels, even though one or more of the children chose to make their presence felt during the investigation.

Although the experiment could not confirm any correlation between infrasound and paranormal experiences in the tunnels, nevertheless it came to the attention of the Association for the Scientific Study of Anomalous Phenomena (ASSAP). The prestigious Michael Bentine Memorial Shield was awarded to Parasearch Chair, David Taylor, for the cutting-edge experimental work conducted in the tunnels beneath Smethwick Swimming Centre.

Much Wenlock Spar Shop, Shropshire

Outbreaks of paranormal activity are often attributed to major changes such as building work in older properties. This certainly seemed to be the case when we were called in to investigate strange goings on in a shop at Much Wenlock in Shropshire. Much Wenlock is a picturesque medieval market town with its ruined Wenlock Priory, Guildhall, and a mix of medieval, Georgian and Victorian buildings. The fine old town clock in the square was donated by Alderman Thomas Cooke in 1897. It is said that he had the clock precisely positioned so as to draw the eye of potential customers to his grocery shop just off the Town Square.

Town Square with Spar shop to the left (Nigel Thompson, CC BY-SA 2.0)

It was Thomas Cooke's old shop that was subject to major rebuilding work in 2002 when the Spar supermarket was enlarged. The shop had been originally built on what was thought to have been a medieval alehouse. Another theory was that the land was once part of Wenlock Abbey cemetery. Whether these theories are correct or not, bits of broken pottery and bones were unearthed during the building work.

Our group was called in because terrified staff were seeing and hearing things that had only started since the building work had commenced. The activity had begun with heavy breathing being heard although at this stage nothing was seen. It quickly escalated to staff seeing supermarket trolleys moving on their own and one shop assistant had felt a hand on her shoulder when there was nobody there. Another supervisor had an unnerving experience when she went into the back of the shop on her own to wash up some cups. She was confronted by a misty figure which blocked her way for a few seconds before fading away.

Arrangements were made to conduct an interview with the manager before the night of our investigation. Nobody else was present at the time. The interview was conducted in a small brick office at the back of the shop on the same side as the building works. On playing back the recording to transcribe the interview a disembodied voice can be clearly heard when the Manager is talking about the shopping trolley she saw moving on its own:

> I could hear this noise. I thought 'what the hell's that'. It was a trolley out there … It was moving from side to side like someone was swinging it.

Interspersed with the interview there is another, different voice, that seems to be commenting on the trolley. The word's 'it's moving' can be clearly heard followed by yet another voice saying, 'time's up'. 🎥 1

Disembodied voices appearing on audio recordings are an example of Electronic Voice Phenomena (EVP). This is a technique used widely by paranormal investigators to try and communicate with any entities present. In this instance though it was totally spontaneous and can clearly be heard commenting on the movement of the shopping trolley.

On the night of our investigation, we tried to recreate the conditions of the interview to see if we could repeat the EVP event but to no avail. Also, it was clear that the little brick office was pretty well insulated from external sounds thus eliminating another possible source of the voices.

The large ground floor area where most of the activity was taking place was mainly empty apart from evidence of recent building works. Up above was another similar sized room which was also being refurbished. There was no access to this room at the time we were there, and it was locked.

Site of the building work and most of the activity

A video camera was set up to continuously record the downstairs area requiring the tapes to be regularly replaced. It was during one such changeover by the author that the following incident occurred:

I had just replaced the tape in the video camera and fortunately double checked that it was recording. Having done this I was walking diagonally across the room when all of a sudden there was a tremendous bang which seemed to be right above me, although I knew there could not possibly have been anyone up in the room above as it was locked off.

We found a small hatch in the ceiling and by placing a chair on a table and steadied by team members [for health and safety!] I was able to shine my torch into the room above. It was empty apart from some house bricks ready to be used. I can only surmise that perhaps it was one of these bricks that was thrown down onto the floor above me. Whatever it was, it was certainly loud! 🎥 2

Nothing else of interest happened that night and the continued building works meant that unfortunately we were not able to repeat our investigation. By the time, the refurbishment had been completed all of the activity had ceased. As far as is known, nothing unusual has been reported from the site since.

📹 1   📹 2

The Starving Rascal

The starving Rascal on Brettell Lane in Amblecote, between Stourbridge and Brierley Hill, is named after the main character in its Victorian ghost story. The activity experienced in later years which we were invited to investigate may or may not be connected with this story, but it is worth relating as central to the character of this Victorian public house.

The Starving Rascal public house

It was wintertime with freezing temperatures and snow on the ground when an old beggar turned up at what was The Dudley Arms. He pleaded with the landlord to be permitted to warm himself by the fire and for some scraps of food and a drink. The landlord, an uncharitable man at the best of times, would have none of it and threw the beggar out into the snow, but not before the old rascal had put a curse on the pub. Having nowhere else to go the old man sat on the step possibly hoping that the landlord would relent and let him in back in. He did not. Instead, the old beggar froze to death that night on the step. It is believed to be his ghost who haunts the building to this day.

Beggars being turned out to die in the snow seems to be something of a theme in the area, as not too far away The Cat Inn at Enville has a very similar ghost story. In this one the beggar, Billy Pitt, is let in to warm himself and is plied with drink but later locked in the village stocks overnight where he froze to death next to the body of his cruelly strangled dog.

Although originally called The Dudley Arms, the pub had been nicknamed 'The Starver' by locals long before the name was officially changed to The Starving Rascal in 1974.

Getting back to more recent times the pub has long been subject to paranormal activity. Customers and staff have reported being touched when there is nobody there. Wet footprints can appear in the pub even on the driest of days. Glasses hanging over the bar can be set swinging as if someone has run their hand along them. Even more intriguing, a hand has been seen reaching out to pick up a pint of beer when there is nobody there. An old man has also been seen around the pub, including sitting at the bar and entering the gentlemen's toilet. Once spotted he simply disappears as soon as the witness looks away. Inexplicable bangs and noises are also heard when the pub is quiet, particularly after closing at night.

It has to be said that pubs are notorious for odd noises occurring, equipment such as coolers and refrigerators operate when needed and other items of essential equipment are timed to turn on and off. Building settle, particularly at night, must also be taken into account which can cause all sorts of bangs and creaks. With experience though it is easy to get to know which sounds are normal – and those that are not.

Right from the start of our investigation at The Starving Rascal odd banging noises could be heard but the exact cause could not be determined. At one point in the bar, we heard a noise akin to someone rapping a walking stick on the bar, possibly expecting service! But it was in the lounge that the rapping really got serious. We were even able to follow it around the room from one side to the other. At one point we thought it might be someone on the outside who knew we were there and was rapping on the windows, even though the building was in darkness. We checked of course and there was nobody anywhere near as might be expected in the early hours of the morning. As often seems to happen though the best was kept till last after we had packed everything away:

Members of the team started seeing what appeared to be a shadowy figure flitting around the lounge area. With so many reflections from shiny surfaces and glass it was impossible to pinpoint exactly, except to say it wasn't any of our small group moving. The lounge had a large ornate mirror on the wall, and as I was packing away some gear a movement caught my eye. It was someone behind me reflected in the mirror. We hadn't turned the lights on for fear of attracting unwanted attention and so it was not possible to make out any details except it seemed to be a man looking directly at me. I instinctively turned around fully expecting one of our team to be standing there. Not only was nobody there, but the rest of the team were the other side of the pub. Needless to say, when I looked back at the mirror the figure had vanished.

In writing up a report of the investigation afterwards it was only possible to confirm that something unusual was certainly going on. Unfortunately, it was not possible to determine exactly what the cause of the activity was, or indeed if it was in any way connected to the Victorian Starving Rascal himself.

In a postscript to this story later on in 2018 a new publican took over and the activity escalated. By now internal CCTV cameras had been installed, and one of them caught a picture coming off the wall and being thrown across the bar. 🎥 1

🎥 1

Stokesay Shropshire

Our local group didn't normally investigate UFO sightings. Ordinarily we would pass such reports onto a local group dealing with such things but every so often a case comes along that seems so incredible that it just has to be followed up. This was just such a case. The location was Stokesay in Shropshire, which although being not far from Craven Arms was clearly going to be a dark sky site. The witness was a retired professional gentleman who had recently relocated from Manchester. He was living within sight of Stokesay Castle, a magnificent medieval fortified manor house and St John the Baptist Church which we knew was allegedly haunted by a misty apparition in the churchyard. But aliens?

St John the Baptist churchyard and Stokesay Castle (Tony Grist, CC0)

The report from the witness stated that on clear nights a large mother ship would appear in the sky and proceed to release what he described as silent triangular 'scout ships'. Occasionally these landed and the occupants could be seen using bright lights in the valley where the witness lived. Stokesay is very sparsely populated and affords far reaching views into the surrounding Shropshire hills. The witness sounded very plausible on the phone and he was absolutely adamant that these events could be witnessed on any clear night. It just had to be investigated further. It was nearly a week later before we had a suitably clear night and duly set out to investigate the alleged phenomena for ourselves. We set out from the Black Country and Telford in a couple of cars. Eager investigators with enough equipment to record any of the reported activity, should it occur. Expectations were high.

The witness's house was one of a pair of nearly new properties situated a bit further along the valley from the church and castle. From the garden at the side of the house there were clear views right along the valley to the Shropshire hills beyond. A noticeable feature of the property was a railway line situated literally at the end of the garden. We met the witness when we arrived and proceeded to obtain further details. He was articulate and well spoken and explained that he had recently exchanged city life in Manchester for peace and quiet in the country. Most of the phenomena had been observed through a large, double-glazed window in the lounge. One thing we did notice was that the witness was very hard of hearing.

Darkness was falling as we arrived, and the weather forecast promised a perfectly clear night. During the interview, the witness suddenly announced that the mother ship had arrived! Sure enough, through the lounge window a large, bright object was clearly visible in the sky just above the hills. Anyone not used to dark night skies devoid of light pollution could easily make the mistake of confusing Sirius, the Dog Star, with an alien mother ship and anyway, we still had the triangular 'scout' ships and the ground activity to look out for. We were not unduly perturbed.

We set up in the garden at the side of the house well away from what little light pollution there was from the houses. Our equipment included various still cameras and a tripod-mounted low light level infra-red video camera with which to record the eagerly anticipated events. We didn't have long to wait. The 'scout' ships soon put in an appearance. We never did determine exactly which airport the passenger jets were flying to and from, but the flight path was certainly a busy one with planes somewhere in the sky virtually all the time. Very often the sound from these high-flying aircraft couldn't be heard down in the valley, and they passed overhead brightly lit but silent. Never mind, we still had the low altitude lights to investigate, so after a coffee we soldiered on.

We didn't have long to wait. Bright aerial lights lower than the surrounding hills were observed around midnight but unfortunately accompanied by the low, deep drone of a heavy transport aircraft. We could only surmise what the plane was doing but given that the SAS were rumoured to train in the area this seemed to be a pretty good bet. One of our number had been brought up in Shropshire and he surmised that at least some of the bright lights seen at ground level could be put down to 'lamping'. This is a tactic often used by poachers using bright lights to dazzle animals in the darkness. We realised that from the witness's point of view inside the house he probably couldn't hear any of this activity outside.

After this most of our party called it a night and departed for home. Two of us decided to brave it out and carry on at least until the coffee in our flasks ran out. Our witness had long since retired to bed and the house was now in darkness, leaving us and a large tripod mounted video camera camped in the garden immediately opposite the driveway.

By about 2.00 am our enthusiasm was waning fast. After standing outside in the cold for most of the night looking at stars and aeroplanes, we were thinking that things could hardly get much worse. That's when the police arrived. As the patrol car drew up the single occupant proceeded to lean across the front seat and wind down the passenger side window. He stared right at us, and we could do nothing but stare back with thoughts of 'we'll never be able to wake the witness', 'how are we going to explain this down the station' and, 'they'll never believe we're only looking for UFOs'. Unbelievably, after staring directly at us he wound the window up again and drove off. Perhaps he couldn't face the paperwork!

After congratulating ourselves on evading arrest and drinking yet another coffee we decided we might as well carry on in the hope of seeing some of the ground level lights which still hadn't been satisfactorily explained. We didn't have long to wait. We became aware of a small yellow glow moving slowly from side to side far in the distance. We watched this light for a few minutes and realised that it was moving towards us. After a while, the light was accompanied by a clattering sound which got louder and louder as whatever it was approached. We stood mesmerised by all this activity, and the sight which eventually greeted us is one that neither of us will ever forget. What came into view was a diesel engine on the railway line. But this was no ordinary diesel. All the metal panels around the locomotive had been removed so it was virtually a skeleton. In addition to this the whole thing was bathed in a bright yellow light showing all the inner workings of the engine. We watched this bizarre spectacle go by in utter amazement. It was only after it had disappeared into the distance that we realised with all the equipment we had ready to record the UFOs, neither of us had thought to take a photograph of the skeleton diesel.

Furthermore, neither of us recalled seeing a driver!

Telford Steam Railway, Horsehay

Telford Steam Railway is not just home to an enthusiastic band of railway volunteers but also the ghost of a former engine driver. As haunted locations go, an engine shed has to be one of the more unusual. Horsehay and Dawley Station fell victim to the Beeching cuts, closing to passengers in 1962 and to freight a couple of years later. In its Victorian heyday the freight side was a hive of industry based around the 'goods transhipment shed'.

Telford Steam Railway engine shed

A Blue Plaque records that 'The Old Loco Shed' was built in 1863 and the odd name 'transhipment shed' referred to the fact that it was used to exchange goods carried on two different gauge tracks which meet within the shed. Here, the Coalbrookdale Company plateways, narrow gauge system met with the Great Western Railway standard gauge line that ran from Wellington to Craven Arms. Telford Steam Railway voluntary group has operated a section of the line since 1976 and has run passenger services and events since 1984.

The focal point for reports of paranormal activity is the old loco shed, used for storage, on the Spring Village side of the station. It is mainly in the early hours of the morning that disembodied footsteps have been heard making their way along the platform. On occasions, witnesses claim to have seen a misty shape accompanying the footsteps. There have also been reports of a solid looking figure wearing the working clothes of an engine driver. Very often though, it is just the sound of footsteps heard echoing along the platform.

The inside platform where the footsteps are heard

We were fortunate to be allowed to investigate the loco shed overnight to be sure of covering the period when the activity is said to take place. The inside of the shed itself was absolutely rammed with railway engineering from a complete diesel shunter and trucks right down to platform furniture and sundry bits of railway memorabilia. The junction of the narrow gauge and standard gauge tracks for the transfer of goods could be clearly seen at one end of the shed and a small office up a short flight of steps over the tracks to the right of the platform was commandeered as our base room for the night.

The building is surprisingly large and there was plenty of room for our small group to spread out and cover all areas. As usual, we were doing 45 minute vigil sessions. Whilst setting up equipment at the far end of the platform, the author had a very strong feeling of being watched from behind. Although this was noted down but not mentioned it was interesting that another investigator had the same feeling in the same place later on in the night. The shed was in darkness apart from when we were using our torches to move around safely or to illuminate something of interest. As the night wore on, we were aware of occasional knocking noises and at one point the sound of something quite heavy being dropped. No amount of searching could determine exactly where these noises were coming from or indeed what, if anything, had been dropped. This short report was written up at the time:

> By about 3.00 am most of our small group had packed up and left taking the majority of the recording equipment with them. However, fellow investigator Gareth and myself decided to spend one last session sitting quietly at the Spring Village platform end of the loco shed. Although there was very little light, we could at least make out the dark shapes of the engines and equipment stored in the shed. After we had sat there for about half an hour, we both heard what sounded like heavy footsteps coming from the other end of the platform. We knew there was nobody down there and looked at each other without saying a word to confirm what we were both hearing. Fully expecting someone to appear out of the darkness, the footsteps continued for a few seconds more and then suddenly stopped. We waited a short while to see if they would begin again and then made our way down the platform to take a look. By this time, we were fully expecting to find someone else in the building, but a thorough search proved this could not possibly have been the case. The outside door we were using was securely locked and we had the key.

At the time, an audio recorder was still running in a different part of the building but unfortunately was too far away to pick up anything conclusive from the platform where we were situated. It always surprises over the years how often something interesting happens either when just setting equipment up, or alternatively when it has been packed away as in this case.

As it happened, we had left a folder of background information behind on the night and so arrangements were made to collect it. The author got talking to one of the railway volunteers who, without prompting, said he hated being alone in the shed at night because he always felt as though he was being watched.

Why should these footsteps and occasional apparition be experienced in the early hours of the morning? Purely on a practical note, the footsteps at least would probably not even be noticed during a normal day. Given the history of the loco shed though it was once busy with freight at all hours of the day and night. Steam engines take hours to prepare from cold and so early morning starts, particularly to coal fire the boilers, would be commonplace. Perhaps it is not an engine driver after all, but a fireman who still sometimes repeats his early morning shifts in the old loco shed.

Tettenhall Towers

If ever a house should be haunted by its former owner it is Tettenhall Towers, now in the grounds of Tettenhall College. It was home to eccentric inventor and philanthropist Lieutenant-Colonel Thomas Thorneycroft. His rank came from voluntary service with the Staffordshire Yeomanry as he was never a professional soldier.

Having closed the increasingly unprofitable ironworks he inherited from his father, the first mayor of Wolverhampton George Thorneycroft, Thomas was able to pursue his various interests as a full-time member of the landed gentry. One of these interests was the Georgian house set in 26 acres of land he bought in 1853. By 1866 he had extended the building and added the towers giving the house its name. On one of the towers Thomas installed a system of semaphore flags so he could communicate with the workers around his estate. Thomas also created his own theatre in the great hall with seating for 500 people which is still in use to this day. The original theatre stage was backed by a tremendous waterfall fed from a tank in one of the towers. He also installed a sprung wooden dance floor which he designed himself. A lover of music and poetry, Thomas was inspired to write of his sprung dance floor:

The oak floor makes a skating rink,
it's on elastic springs.
So when you dance, you're apt to think,
you're fluttering on wings.

He filled his house with hunting trophies and was obsessed with the design of water closets (toilets), sanitation, heating, and ventilation. One of his numerous interests was flying machines which he would launch from the top of the towers and, if local legend is to be believed, piloted by terrified servants! Thomas seems to have been fascinated by flight as he was nearly killed during an ascent in a hydrogen balloon named Dudley Castle from the grounds of the Molyneux Hotel in 1882. The balloon initially failed to gain height and nearly crashed into an ironworks. His response was to promptly invent a device for steering balloons and to offer advice to future air travellers including what to wear. Colonel Thorneycroft died in 1903 as a result of recklessly insisting on riding a mighty water chute set up for an exhibition in West Park, Wolverhampton. He was 81 years old at the time.

Tettenhall Towers

Tettenhall Towers is the epitome of a haunted house with its labyrinth of cellars, passageways, stairways, and the seriously strange rooms upstairs known as the Doll's House. Hardly surprising perhaps, given his attachment to the building in life, that the ghost of Colonel Thorneycroft himself is said to still wander around his former home and dark, shadowy figures are to be seen flitting around the many rooms in this most mysterious of places. The upstairs Doll's House is perhaps the most unnerving with unexplained footsteps being heard, objects getting thrown around and the sounds of children's voices echoing through the claustrophobic rooms.

Our investigation there started with a health and safety talk from our host. Bizarrely, we were instructed not to, 'lick the wallpaper' in the Doll's House. As amusing as this may sound it was in fact a deadly serious warning particularly in the 19th century. Arsenic based pigments enabled vibrant greens, yellows, and blues to be used in wallpapers and was immensely popular throughout the Victorian era. Tragically, it was often younger children who suffered most from this accidental and often fatal poisoning.

As per usual for our investigation team, we split into small groups and rotated around what we considered to be the active areas of the building spending 45 minutes in each. Throughout the night there were odd noises which couldn't quite be pinpointed including a single bark from a dog down in the cellar complex. Needless to say, there was no dog down there or indeed anywhere else in the building.

Having been in the cellar when the dog barked hopes were high especially when the person responsible for the building overnight was able to confirm there should be no dogs in the school grounds and certainly not in the building itself.

After this, it was our turn for two of us to investigate the Doll's House upstairs. It was quite a squeeze for us to move between the rooms as everything was just smaller than it should have been. The whole area was in total darkness which didn't help with having to move around by torchlight. We were told it was once the servant's quarters, but I rather doubt this. I think it much more likely that it was built for Colonel Thorneycroft's children. Although clearly eccentric he was a devoted family man and had a total of nine children between 1848 and 1869.

We crawled through a space into one of the rooms and sat ourselves down for the 45-minute vigil session. About halfway through our time there we clearly heard footsteps coming up the wooden stairs into the Doll's House and someone moving around in the room right next to ours. As it is a strict rule that people don't move about between investigation areas, we assumed that somebody must have good reason to be looking for us. Fully expecting someone to make themselves known we called out to them. There was no answer. The room was empty and silent when we looked in. Furthermore, having heard someone clearly coming up the stairs there was no sound of anyone going back down again.

Careful checking confirmed that everyone could be accounted for, and nobody had been anywhere near the Doll's House or indeed on the stairs at the time.

The Belgrave Triangle

The term 'The Belgrave Triangle' was coined by my good friend, the late Terry Hewitt. It referred to an area of old Belgrave Village, now a part of Leicester City, which caught the imagination of the world's media in early 1999. The 'triangle' consisted of Belgrave Hall, St Peter's Churchyard next door, and the Talbot public house nearly opposite.

Belgrave Hall

Our investigations concentrated mainly on Belgrave Hall itself and the Talbot pub although weather permitting, we always included vigil sessions in the churchyard. The reason for all the attention though was piece of security camera footage from December 1998 which appeared to show what looked like a lady in Victorian dress on the path running across the rear of Belgrave Hall. 🎥 1

Belgrave Hall from the rear where the anomaly was recorded

With the footage having hit the headlines, speculation began immediately as to who she might be. Three prosperous families had been associated with

Belgrave Hall. It was built by merchant Edmund Craddock in the early 1700s and was later owned by the High Sherriff of Leicestershire, William Vann. However, interest fell on the better known Ellis family who had acquired Belgrave Hall in 1845. John Ellis was a Leicester MP and had been instrumental in bringing the railway to Leicester in 1833. He had several children and five of his daughters, known as the 'Belgrave Sisters' continued to live on in the house after their father's death. They were all involved in the early days of the women's suffrage movement to obtain the vote. In particular, the press dropped on Charlotte Ellis as the most likely candidate to be haunting Belgrave Hall. She was said to have been the feistiest of the five sisters and sometimes portrayed by a staff member in costume. Some quite famous mediums became involved but given the amount of history and speculation as to the identity of the ghost that had previously taken place, it is difficult to know how much they had been influenced by previous knowledge.

The image on the security camera was in fact only a small part of activity that had been experienced at Belgrave Hall over a long period of time. On occasions, when a staff member was dressed as Charlotte, visitors had asked why there were two actresses in period costume. There was ever only one. Olfactory phenomena in the form of cooking smells were common but often it would only be staff who would realise that there was no actual bread being baked or meat being cooked. On one occasion, the landlady from the Talbot pub opposite casually commented to Stuart Warburton, the curator, that someone must have been working late as the curtains were drawn and a light was on in one of the upstairs rooms. It turned out that the curtains are always left open and any movement inside the house would have triggered the alarms. One of the most interesting sightings is that of a lady in a long terracotta dress who has been seen on a number of occasions in the house coming down the stairs and disappearing along the passage towards the kitchen.

When news of the security camera video recording broke, both Stuart Warburton the curator and Leicester City Council, to their credit, were keen to get the anomaly investigated professionally. The Association for the Scientific Study of Anomalous Phenomena (ASSAP) became involved and so too did Parasearch, an ASSAP accredited regional group together with others such as Terry Hewitt who, being Leicester based, was the obvious choice to lead the investigation.

The initial approach taken was to examine the security camera system and see if the recorded anomaly could be reliably replicated. It turned out that the system was new, and computer controlled. Sensors around the building would trigger infrared lights and cameras if tripped. An added security feature was that, in the event of a fault, the system would record the last image frame for a few seconds before resetting. There had been various theories put forward as to what the image might be and it has to be said that ghost was at the bottom of our list. It was decided to test out these theories. A ladder was placed up against the security camera in question, and a live monitor was observed from down below. The author's theory was that it was a bat that had created the image:

I had a copy of the footage taken from the security camera and showed it to a wildlife expert friend. His opinion, given the shape, was that the camera had picked up a bat. For the purposes of the experiment, I had borrowed a rubber bat from my daughter Sophie under strict instructions that it must be returned intact! Armed with this, I was first to climb the ladder and dangle the bat in front of the camera. It seemed to impress the ITV news crew that were filming it but not so the ASSAP investigators watching the screen. It looked nothing like the anomaly. Next up the ladder was ASSAP Chair, Phil Walton, with a bag of assorted leaves from the garden. One of these, an oak leaf, fitted the bill perfectly and recorded an image very close to the original anomaly.

The sequence of events could now be put together to explain the anomaly. An animal, probably a fox, had run up the side of the house and triggered multiple sensors. This switched on the infrared lights and enabled the camera to start recording an image. By pure coincidence, a leaf was falling in front of the lens at the exact same instant the computer system got overloaded with inputs from the sensors. The image was frozen for a few seconds whilst the computer sorted itself out, and then continued recording. The result was the video sequence and anomaly (oak leaf) which had created so much media interest. Stuart Warburton and Leicester City Council were satisfied that a good job had been done. However, that did not stop other groups investigating including ISPR with Larry Montz and Derek Acorah, who produced a one-hour programme on Belgrave Hall. Terry Hewitt and I did a number of radio and television broadcasts from Belgrave. On one occasion a Japanese film crew came to interview us for Asahi Channel 10 TV. Apparently, our voices were dubbed into Japanese!

One of the vigil sessions in Belgrave Hall

Although the anomaly had been solved to our satisfaction, we were still interested in investigating Belgrave Hall in conjunction with St Peter's Churchyard and the Talbot pub opposite. Staff were still experiencing unusual events such as a child of about five or six crossing the lawn very early one morning when Belgrave Hall was shut to the public. A search revealed no trace of a child. The music box in an empty room was suddenly found to be playing even though nobody had been anywhere near. Belgrave Hall was always atmospheric but not very active from an investigation point of view, beyond footsteps from upstairs and a loud female sigh heard on one occasion. If anything, the Talbot pub opposite was far more active.

St Peter's Churchyard

The original church of St Peter can be traced back to the thirteenth century. However, it is the churchyard which is known for its reports of ghostly activity. A former employee of the Talbot pub had a typical experience whilst walking past the church with her friend. They both saw a lady in the churchyard wave to them as they walked past. Nothing too unusual in that, except this particular lady then walked straight through a tombstone and promptly disappeared.

With the permission of the vicar and weather permitting, we would always spend at least one vigil session in the churchyard. During one of these investigations, Julie Hunt saw a stationary white figure standing at the rear of the church. The apparition was there just long enough for Julie to fire off two shots with her Canon SLR film camera before it disappeared.

The results were awaited with great anticipation as it is extremely rare to see an apparition long enough to be able to take a photograph. Unfortunately, not just the photographs in the churchyard but the entire film turned out to be ruined when it was returned from the developers. Time and time again it seems that ghosts are simply camera shy!

The Talbot Public House

Originally a coaching inn, the Talbot is thought to date back to the sixteenth century although it underwent major alterations in the 1950s after a fire.

The Talbot public house (David Hallam Jones, CC BY-SA 2.0)

Like most pubs of this age, local stories are a mix of legend and perhaps some facts. In the case of the Talbot, it is reputed to have provided a last meal for condemned prisoners on their way to be hung at Red Hill Gallows. The bodies would often be dissected by doctors but probably not in a mortuary attached to the Talbot as legend suggests.

The Talbot claims a number of ghosts including a man in black with a heavy purse and a cape, a former landlord's son who sits and swings his legs by the fireside, and a former owner called Mary Dawson who wears mourning black and scowls at staff and customers through a window in the bar.

When we were there, the landlord and landlady would trust us with the keys to lock up after a night's investigation. They would go off to bed upstairs and we would hear nothing further from them. The Talbot had two bars at right angles to each other, a larger lounge bar and a smaller room with a pool table. The door to the Pool Rom was opposite a back door to the pub and in the passageway a straight staircase led up to a corridor with bedrooms either side.

During our first investigation at the pub, after the landlord and landlady had gone to bed, Terry Hewitt and another investigator opted to go upstairs whilst the author and fellow investigator Gareth were in the Pool Room:

> The pub was completely quiet but after a few minutes we heard a bang, like something heavy being dropped from upstairs above our heads. This was followed by loud footsteps, sounds like furniture being dragged and more loud bangs. We assumed it was something the other pair of investigators were doing upstairs. At the end of the 45-minute vigil session when they came down, I remember saying that we would never be invited here again with all the noise they had been making. It turned out that not only had they sat quietly for the whole time but they also had not heard any of the bangs, footsteps and dragging sounds that we had been listening to downstairs. The landlord and landlady had not been disturbed by any of this either.

On subsequent investigations at the Talbot, we made sure that contact microphones were attached to the ceiling of the Pool Room. Of course, the noises were never repeated for us again.

It was on another of our investigations that Michael Lewis, National Investigations Co-ordinator for ASSAP at the time, saw his first ghost after decades of investigating. The following description is reproduced with Mike's kind permission from his 2013 book *Conclusions of a Parapsychologist*:

Terry Hewitt was upstairs changing the tapes on his video camera, the other two investigators [including the author] were doing the same in the lounge bar. From my position I had a clear view of the saloon bar, and also along behind the bar to the rear lobby area through the open door at the end of the counter. From this lobby stairs lead to the upper floor, although they face away from the bar. The bar lights were on, and early morning sunshine provided clear illumination.

Suddenly I saw the figure of a man pass across the doorway at the end of the counter, directly in my line of vision. This surprised me, as Terry could be heard upstairs, and the other two investigators were talking in the lounge bar. Anticipating that the man would go through the door in front of him into the saloon bar, I transferred my gaze to the bar side of the door (which was open). Sure enough, as large as life and bold as brass, he walked across the bar and stood by the front entrance lobby door. We stared at each other. Each seemed to be thinking "What are you doing here?" Annoyance came over me, as I assumed he must be the pub cleaner and that meant an early end to a fruitless vigil. He then turned and walked back across the bar. My training kicked in, and I observed him closely, as well as I might, being no more than six feet away!

The man was tall and thin, with a duffle or anorak coat and dark trousers. His gait rolled slightly, and he was in no hurry. The coat was rather large and hung off him, as did the hood attached to the coat. He walked into what was then the Pool Room next to the saloon bar, and out of sight. Had he turned left to retrace his steps, he would have literally bumped into Terry Hewitt who was descending the stairs at that moment. Realising that I had the keys to the pub in my pocket and was responsible for the security of the building, I decided I had to challenge him, hoping not to make too much a fool of myself with what I had every reason to believe was a member of the pub's staff.

By this time Terry was at the foot of the stairs and I told him there was a man in the Pool Room. "That's the Ghost!" he exclaimed, and so confident was I that it was a mortal man I had seen, I responded "Well, that would be the biggest turn up for the book there's ever been!". We entered the Pool Room and immediately saw that it was quite empty. For me, it was a defining moment (perhaps the defining moment, who knows?) in my life. I then knew what a lottery winner must feel like. The elation I felt was beyond words, matched by Terry's chagrin at missing the apparition by mere seconds, and the astonishment of my two colleagues at what had happened just outside the line of their vision. By correlation with numerous other sightings of apparitions in the pub, we deduced that I had seen the ghost of a pub regular from the nineteen sixties who frequented the saloon bar in death as well as life, on one occasion going up to the bar, presenting one shilling and threepence and asking for a half of mild (beer)!

Having gone into the Pool Room there was no way out except the way he went in. Both Terry and myself had missed the apparition literally by seconds, but can certainly confirm the story as related by Mike himself above.

For all his work organising what was one of ASSAP's biggest investigations ever mounted, the late Terry Hewitt was very deservedly awarded the Michael Bentine Memorial Shield.

🎥 1

The Woodman, Gornal Wood

Many pubs, particularly older ones such as The Woodman dating back to the 1850s, will claim a certain amount of low-level poltergeist type activity if asked. Perhaps this is something to do with the sheer number of people, and the range of emotions, experienced within their walls over the years. Usually, it is low level activity. Things get moved and reappear in odd places or inexplicably go missing altogether, knocks and bangs are heard, furniture gets moved and that kind of thing. Not so for a time at the Woodman in Gornal Wood near Dudley.

The Woodman public house Gornalwood

When we were invited to investigate the strange goings on, poltergeist activity was being witnessed by both staff and customers. Usually, extreme poltergeist activity such as this is short lived and so it proved to be here. Our group was fortunate to be able to investigate before it subsided altogether. Initial interviews with the landlord, bar staff and some regular customers revealed what had been going on at the pub.

On one occasion an almighty crash had been heard in the upstairs kitchen. All of the plates kept in there were found to have been smashed – all except one which was discovered intact in the middle of the floor. One of the most remarkable occurrences, reported by both staff and customers, involved objects being lifted and moved by unseen hands. A member of the bar staff told us she had watched a beer glass levitate from behind the bar and land on the floor upright without breaking. Astonished customers had even witnessed full pint glasses being lifted off bar tables and placed on the floor without so much as a drop of beer being spilt! Despite this sounding extremely far-fetched, the author together with other witnesses experienced much the same thing with a heavy glass cake stand cover (see the entry for the Black Country Living Museum).

Another customer had the frightening experience of seeing a heavy metal spirit measure being thrown at his head from behind the bar. Fortunately, poltergeist activity rarely, if ever, results in injury and so it was in this case. Having been clearly thrown, the spirit measure dropped harmlessly to the floor before hitting the customer. On another occasion one of the large pub keys went missing. A search all over the pub was made without success. The following morning, the key was found lying right in the centre of a freshly made bed.

Activity was also carrying on after hours when the pub was shut up for the night and everyone had gone to bed. Numerous times in the early hours of the morning the pub alarm would go off to warn of an intruder. There was never anybody there. Even more bizarrely, after tidying the darts away at the end of a night, in the morning they would often be found left out again, or even stuck in the dartboard as though someone had played a game. The bar television was always unplugged at night only to be often found plugged in again the following morning.

On the night of our investigation, hopes were high, and we were not to be disappointed. The first unusual experience occurred fairly early on. We had split into pairs to cover the bars and the cellar areas. The author and a colleague were in one side of the main bar whilst another pair of investigators were positioned in an alcove seating area at the other end of the pub.

During our 45-minute vigil sessions we always observed silence. Any talking for any reason was noted down on our vigil recording sheets. Shortly into the 45-minute session we could clearly hear talking. It was not quite loud enough to be able to discern what was being said, but it was definitely people talking. We made our way to the other side of the bar to ask the other team if they were talking and it was not them. In fact, they had assumed that it had been us. There was nobody else in the vicinity that it could have been, and the talking had ceased by the time we returned back to our area. Others would hear the same talking in the bar during the night although the source was never determined.

Throughout the night doors which had been opened for us would be found to be locked, and then later on opened again. It was almost as though someone, or something, was deliberately playing with us. At the end of our investigation around 3.00 am our small group was gathered in the bar for the final debriefing session. I was standing at the back and distinctly heard someone behind me in the corridor leading to the cellar door. I immediately went to see who it was but of course there was nobody there. We had been using the cellar all night for our investigations so there was absolutely no reason why the door should now suddenly be locked. The last thing we did before leaving the pub was to check the cellar door again. It was unlocked.

We did not use mediums on our investigations unless it was under strictly controlled circumstances (see Drakelow Tunnels and the Theatre on the Steps) but a medium brought in by the landlord had previously said there were two mischievous children haunting the pub. Who knows?

The Theatre on the Steps

D o multiple witnesses to a seemingly paranormal event necessarily all experience the same thing? The author found himself ideally placed to answer this particular question late one night at Bridgnorth in Shropshire during a charity ghost hunt.

Bridgnorth with the Theatre in the centre halfway up Stoneway Steps

The picturesque and historic market town of Bridgenorth is home to one of the country's most unusual theatres. Aptly named The Theatre on the Steps it is situated midway along the ancient Stoneway Steps which connects Low Town with High Town in Bridgnorth. Nowadays passengers can take the Bridgnorth Cliff Railway which dates back to 1892 and is England's steepest inland funicular railway. The only access to the theatre though is by climbing up or down the steep flight of steps.

The building dates back to 1709 and has not always been a theatre. It was originally built as a Presbyterian Chapel and later became a Congregational

Church. Known locally as the Stoneway Chapel, it eventually became the Theatre on the Steps in the early 1960s.

Main entrance on the Stoneway Steps

The building has a long history of paranormal activity. The front doors open onto inner doors which in turn open out into the foyer bar and a staircase leading up to the balcony. Much of the ghostly activity is centred on this area. A lady in green is said to sweep down the staircase and through the foyer. She has also been seen on the balcony and in the auditorium but is sometimes described as being a grey figure. The foyer staircase up to the auditorioum has a landing halfway up. This is where the ghost of the lady in green or grey has been seen and possibly by the author:

On one occasion I was on my own in the foyer setting up video equipment ready for an overnight investigation. Everyone else was in the auditorium. Thinking I was alone, I was suddenly startled by a movement on the stairs. A female figure was just disappearing around the corner on the landing. Logically, it had to be one of the ladies in our team. It wasn't. Further investigation proved that nobody had been upstairs at the time, and everyone was indeed in the auditorium.

Unfortunately, the camera I had been setting up was not switched to record. At different times we heard loud rapping noises in the bar area and on one occasion a vaguely human shimmering shape was experienced by three of our team members.

The foyer bar is also home to strange light effects which have been witnessed by different people and on numerous occasions.

Area of the Foyer Bar where light effects were seen

During an investigation at the theatre the author experienced such an effect which can best be described as a door opening from the area of the auditorium reflecting light onto the opposite wall. Nothing too strange in that you may think except that at the time no doors had been opened or closed and all the lights were turned off in both the foyer and the adjoining auditorium.

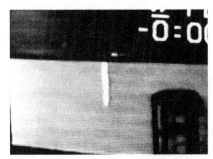 

Two of the light effects recorded in the darkened foyer

On one occasion we were able to conduct another controlled investigation this time with three mediums who were visiting the area from the north of England. The method used was similar in that they had no knowledge of where they were going, each medium was allocated a 'guide' with a digital recorder and finally they were separated from each other until the experiment was completed.

> Two of the mediums provided information which might be expected from a theatre. For example, 'great emotion', 'people in old fashioned clothes', 'a former manager still here' and similar observations. As luck would have it, I was paired with Myra who turned out to be much more interesting. It is important to note that although the building started life as a Chapel, it's unique location and subsequent conversion work to make it a theatre has removed all vestiges of its former life.
>
> Myra made no mention of anything 'theatrical' and was insistent that religious ceremonies had taken place here. Playing Devil's Advocate, I did my best to suggest that this was probably related to performances over the years. Myra would have none of it and insisted that the ceremonies, namely births, marriages, and deaths, were genuine and definitely not play acting.

Was there some clue that we had missed outside or inside the building? I don't think so as we arrived in the dark anyway and alterations to turn it into a theatre had removed everything that might have given a clue as to its origins. Not only that, Myra also correctly described the activity which had been experienced in the building and the locations.

On another occasion, the author and a colleague had agreed to assist with helping a group of nurses who had organised a charity ghost hunt event overnight at the theatre. Not expecting anything paranormal to occur may even have contributed to the following experience:

> I had arrived a little early and walked up the steps from Low Town to meet up with the group. When I reached the theatre, a lady called Wendy and her teenage daughter were waiting outside for the event to begin. We got chatting, and whilst we were talking, we could hear the group on the inside of the building. I banged on the door and continued chatting while we waited to be let in. After a few minutes

we had still not been let in but the noise from inside had got louder. We could hear people moving about and occasionally talking and laughing. I banged the door even louder the second time and remember commenting that it was about time they let us in.

After a few more minutes we had still not been let in and, on hearing someone opening the inner door just on the other side of where we were standing, I went to bang on the door once again. Just as I was about to do this Wendy said, "Wait a minute, some people are coming down the steps". Sure enough, a group of about twenty ladies led by a man carrying a lantern and a key on a large metal ring were heading down towards us together with my colleague. As the door was unlocked and opened, we were still expecting to see the people we had so clearly heard inside the building. It was only as the code to disable the intruder alarm was being tapped in that we realised something was not right. As the charity event had been widely advertised my initial thought was that some people had secreted themselves inside the theatre in order to scare the nurses later on. However, a thorough search of the building revealed that it had been empty all the time we had been waiting outside and if not, the alarm would surely have been triggered.

Without realising it at the time it was happening we had clearly witnessed something strange. In order to record all of the details, I interviewed Wendy and her daughter separately and before they were able to discuss the experience between themselves. The results were interesting. It turned out that both Wendy and I had heard people moving about, doors opening and closing and the sounds of people talking and laughing. Wendy's teenage daughter on the other had had heard the movement noises and the doors but nothing of the people talking and laughing. This begs the question as to how much of our experience was objective (actual) and how much was subjective (personal)? If the digital recorder in my bag had been switched on at the time, we might have had the answer!

This is by no means the first time that people have been heard inside the theatre when there is supposed to be no-one there. On occasions, staff preparing for a performance have assumed people have gained entry to the bar area only to discover the doors securely locked and the foyer empty.

No wonder the theatre hosts the Bridgnorth Halloween ghost walks.

The Tontine Hotel

Research for *Haunted Hostelries of Shropshire* took me to Ironbridge and the Tontine Hotel. Opened in 1784, it was built by a consortium which included members of the Darby family. The unusual name stems from the method used to fund the building. Investors received interest on their investment, but as each one died, the interest was shared amongst the survivors and eventually the last surviving investor received all. Investors profited from the death of their fellows which even in the 18th century was regarded as a somewhat macabre way to make money.

The Tontine Hotel Ironbridge

Room 5 is said to be haunted by murderer Frank Griffin, who spent a desperate few days in there trying to hide from the police in 1950 after killing 74 year-old Jane Edge, the landlady of the Queen's Head Hotel in Ketley. She had caught him stealing and his story when arrested was that he had only pushed her out of the way. Nevertheless, the fall killed her, and Griffin was tried for her murder. He met his fate at the end of a rope in Shrewsbury Prison on January 4th, 1951.

Room 5 where murderer Frank Griffin stayed

Room 5 is subject to feelings of intense cold and the taps in the bathroom have been known to turn themselves on in the middle of the night. Not only that, but people staying in the room have had the intense feeling of a presence in there with them and even more terrifying the feeling that something was strangling them. A workman who was doing a repair in Room 5 experienced the sudden extreme cold and refused to return to finish the job.

Other rooms too are subject to activity. Footsteps have been heard outside Room 9 when there is nobody there. The figure of a man has been seen in Room 2 passing through a wardrobe where at one time there used to be a door. An American guest in Room 4 reported feeling someone sit down on the bed even though there was nobody else there.

All this activity attracted a group of student doctors and nurses for a charity overnight ghost hunt. They booked Room 5 with the intention of staying up all night. The following morning, they came down to breakfast and asked to apologise to the people with the little girl. They had been making a fair amount of noise during the night and had heard their little girl crying.

The breakfast chef told them not to worry. "We didn't have any other residents but yourselves in last night".

Whilst researching for the *Haunted Hostelries of Shropshire* book I had permission to take some photographs in the haunted rooms:

I started in Room 5, and it was pleasantly warm even though it was February because the central heating was on. As I was taking the pictures, I stood partially in the bathroom to get a wider view. The door was already open, and I noticed how freezing cold the bathroom was. At the time I remember putting this down to the time of year and I did not pay it too much attention to it. Having taken another couple of pictures from different positions in the room I decided to try and get a wider-angle view from the bathroom again.

There could have been no more than a couple of minutes between the shots but the temperature in the bathroom now felt pleasantly warm, exactly like the rest of the room. Nothing had changed, no doors or windows had been opened or closed but the intense feeling of icy cold had gone, to be replaced by the pleasant warmth you would expect in a comfortable modern hotel bedroom.

Wem Town Hall

It is difficult to imagine the scene of utter destruction which took place on the 19th of November 1995 when the original Wem Town Hall was engulfed in flames and burned to the ground. Amongst the crowds gathered that night to watch was amateur photographer, Tony O'Rahilly. One of the photographs, taken on black and white film with his 200mm lens, appeared to show a young girl standing in the doorway to the fire escape of the fiercely burning building. Since then, the Wem "Girl in the flames" picture (Figure 1) has become one of the best known and widely published ghost photographs ever taken.

Figure 1. Wem Town Hall 'Girl in the flames'
(Copyright Fortean/O'Rahilly/TopFoto)

The picture very quickly became linked with the story of Jane Churm who, in March 1677, allegedly started a great fire in Wem with a candle. Whilst collecting some stored wood for the fire, the fourteen-year-old girl placed her candle too close to the thatched roof. The roof caught fire and many buildings in Wem, including the Market House, were completely destroyed. The fire was said to have been visible for many miles around. Since then, local legend associated her guilt-ridden ghost with the old Wem Town Hall and she was reputedly seen on a number of occasions. One such incident involved two workmen in the old hall doing some refurbishment work who reported being terrified by a ghostly figure shrouded in a swirling mist which passed directly in front of them.

Tony's picture received extensive media coverage and ASSAP regional group, Parasearch, were first on the scene to investigate. Wem is a small market town in Shropshire to the north of Shrewsbury. On our first visit there to view the remains of the Town Hall we had arranged to meet a local reporter from the Shropshire Star who had the original negative in their possession. Our small group duly arrived outside the Town Hall on the High Street and were just wondering how we would recognise the reporter. We needn't have worried. A gentleman walked straight up to us and said, "You'll be the Ghostbusters then". He wasn't the only one either to recognise us. Whilst doing a bit of background research in the local library, a little boy, probably no more than about five or six, came up to us and demanded to know where our Ghostbusters uniforms were. So as not to shatter his illusions we said they were all in the wash! One of the most memorable incidents occurred whilst we were trying to ascertain the likely height of the girl in the picture. Customers from a nearby pub piled out onto the street and gave us a somewhat drunken rendition of the Ghostbuster's theme. So much for trying to keep a low profile.

Various experts were called on to give an opinion including Dr Vernon Harrison of ASSAP. He concluded that whilst the negative appeared not to have been tampered with, the figure was most likely burning debris which by chance appeared to look like a little girl. A classic case of Pareidolia in fact. Dr Harrison did suggest that, 'it could be a burning plank of wood though'.

A BBC programme made at the time had a copy of the photograph analysed by experts at the National Museum of Photography, Film, and Television in Bradford (now the National Media Museum). Paul Thompson and Will Stapp concluded that the image had been manipulated. Indeed, Thompson detected what he thought were scan lines, 'as though the image consisted of a photo of a face on a video screen pasted into the picture of the fire'.

It has to be said that there were no witnesses to the girl being in the flames including Tony himself who claimed he only discovered her presence when he developed the film. The fire service recorded a video of the blaze, and this too showed no sign of the little girl or indeed the burning debris which could have created the illusion according to Dr Harrison.

The author met with Tony O'Rahilly at the time who maintained that he was as curious as anyone as to how the girl had come to appear on his picture. For this reason, he was more than willing for the original negative to be examined by experts which is how Dr Harrison got involved. Tony showed me his little darkroom set up in a shed behind his house where he did all of his own developing and printing. One slightly odd aspect was that Tony claimed he could not find any of the negatives preceding or following the image of the girl which had been cut out from the rest of the strip. Preceding and following exposures from the same negative strip of the town hall burning down would have helped to authenticate the image. Tony did have other pictures of the burning building however, including the one reproduced here (Figure 2) which he gave me at the time. As with the fire service video there is no indication of burning debris creating any kind of illusion. Having always maintained he was a very amateur photographer this other picture did hold an interesting clue which I didn't realise at the time. A small advertising sticker on the back suggests he was a bit more than the amateur photographer he claimed to be and more than capable of producing copies of photographs and producing internegs. The very technique digital imaging specialist Steve Potter would later suggest was used to produce the enigmatic picture. I like to think Tony was trying to tell me something!

Figure 2. Previously unpublished picture by Tony O'Rahilly & the advertising sticker

It was in 2007 that Steve Potter examined my own high-quality image which had been taken directly from the original negative by the Shropshire Star in 1995. Steve noted a denser area behind the figure that could have been due to, "a thicker area of the original negative". He concluded that, "this image could be a selective enlargement which then was re-touched either on the print or by using an interneg of the figure being sandwiched between the original negative or even a copy negative". A negative created from a manipulated photograph in other words. However, Steve was able to discount the scan line theory finding that, "the lines on the print do not suggest scan lines of an image photographed from a television screen but scratch lines made by dust and dirt in the camera's back, a common problem in 35mm cameras". It has to be noted that Steve had access to digital image analysis techniques simply not available to the experts, including Dr Harrison, who were consulted in 1995.

The story now moves to the 17th of May 2010, when a report by Toby Neal appeared in the Shropshire Star. A retired engineer, Brian Lear, had spotted a little girl bearing a striking resemblance to the girl in the flames on a postcard of Wem High Street dating from 1922 (Figure 3). She can be seen standing in a doorway on the bottom left-hand side of the postcard.

Figure 3. Postcard from 1922 with the little girl on the left discovered by Brian Lear

Closer analysis of both images side by side (Figure 4) reveals that the folds in her bonnet and dress are identical as is the narrow sash she is wearing around her waist. The little girl's right hand and thumb is also clearly visible in both images. There can be little doubt that this is the source of the picture which has intrigued so many people for so long.

Figure 4. Wem Town Hall girl is on the right

Tony O'Rahilly sadly passed away in 2005 but having met and talked with him I am convinced he believed he was acting in the best interests of Wem by bringing the town hall fire and the story of Jane Churm to the attention of the world's media. It certainly caused a sensation at the time and who knows, perhaps Tony's picture helped to focus attention on the rebuilding of Wem Town Hall which was opened in 2000.

Even though the 'girl in the flames' has now been satisfactorily explained, what was it that prompted Tony to produce the picture in the first place? The association with Jane Churm in the media had come about after the photograph was made public. The answer may lie with the ghostly figure seen by the workmen in the old Town Hall shortly before the fire and reported in the local paper. Could this have been the ghost of Jane Churm come to warn of another fire and the inspiration for Tony O'Rahilly's enigmatic picture?

West Bromwich Manor House

S ince being taken over by Sandwell Museum Service, the name has reverted to Bromwich Hall. This was a moated manor house, and the half-timbered black and white buildings still retain the original moat and chapel. The oldest part of the house, the medieval timber-framed hall, dates back to 1270 and was built by Richard de Marnham. This historic building passed through many hands and was altered and added to particularly in the 18th century. A decline in fortunes saw the Manor House converted to tenements and nearly demolished in the 1940s. Fortunately it was saved by West Bromwich Corporation, restored, and used for many years as a pub and a restaurant before becoming a museum.

Bromwich Hall the West Bromwich Manor House Museum

As might be expected with a building of this age there are numerous stories of hauntings. One of these concerns the sighting of a medieval knight who may have been the victim of a murder in 1293 when Richard de Marnham's son, Nicholas, was killed in the grounds of the hall. The murderer was Bertram de Marnham, his own brother, who was found not guilty. If it is Richard, he is not alone as mysterious hooded figures resembling monks have been seen around the moat. Staff have been startled by an old lady and gentleman peering out of an upstairs window after locking up. Apparitions have also been seen in different parts of the building, but especially in the Great Hall and the upstairs area known as the Solar Bar when the Manor House was in use as a pub.

Before the pub closed for good and became a museum, our paranormal research group was able to mount a number of investigations just at the time when the landlord and staff were experiencing regular activity. Part of it may have been that they were often in the perfect position to observe the upstairs area known as the Solar Bar. This was a narrow room that lead to further seating in adjacent upstairs rooms situated at one end of the Great Hall and accessed by a staircase at the side. At the other end of the Great Hall, was the main bar with seating and tables in between. It was from here that serving staff would regularly see a figure walking through the Solar Bar when they knew there was nobody up there. Often, this would be before the pub opened to customers.

Speaking to staff before our first investigation, the figure in the Solar Bar had been seen shortly before we arrived. Later on, at approximately 3.30 am one of our team saw a shadow appear on the wall opposite where she was sitting. A head and shoulders were clearly seen on one of the white painted panels in between the dark wooden beams.

On our next investigation, the author and another team member, Jen, went up into the Solar Bar to see if the shadow would reappear for us.

Around 3.00 am we started a 45-minute vigil session in the Solar Bar sitting opposite where the shadow had been seen on our previous investigation. This time we had a portable video recorder to record the event if it occurred again. It did. We both had vigil record sheets and I remember Jen looking down to start writing something on her sheet. As she did so, a very definite shadow of someone suddenly appeared on the white panel opposite and to my left. The head and shoulders particularly were clearly visible. Before I could alert Jen, the shadow had faded.

When we played back the video recording, we were very disappointed to see that because the bar was so narrow it had not recorded the panel to the left, only the one directly ahead. We spent a great deal of time trying to reproduce a shadow on the wall in the same place. It was simply not possible to replicate it, and nobody else was upstairs with us at the time.

On subsequent investigations we always made sure that team members were in the Solar Bar around the appropriate time, but the shadow never reappeared for us again.

Very often, when something is about to happen, the atmosphere will seem to change, and senses will become more alert. This was the case in the Great Hall when a long-haired solid looking figure wearing a white top and some sort of brown jacket caught the eye of one of our investigators. It seemed to be that once he realised he had been seen, he simply vanished. The first thought was that he had been an intruder, and where he was standing it did look as though there might have once been a door but not in our time.

Often, as in the case of the shadows and the figure in the hall, paranormal events are fleeting and allow little time for observation, but not always. Beneath the Solar Bar was another bar with a seating area towards the front of the building. At the end of this bar, was a tiny wood framed room accessed up a step and through a narrow door. The windows in this room were of old fashioned dark yellow glass and a large wooden door led back into the Great Hall. It was in here that the author, and fellow investigator Gareth, witnessed a display of small pure white lights.

> The room was in complete darkness and small white lights started to appear randomly on the walls. We checked ourselves to make sure it was nothing we were doing and even looked to see if they could be coming from outside despite the yellow glass. This strange display of white lights lasted for a good minute or so before stopping. Despite having the time to look, we could find no possible explanation for these lights appearing as they did.

The wooden door from this little room leading into the Great Hall had knot holes in it big enough to just see through. As the little room was dark it was possible to see through to the other side where it was a little bit lighter. Whilst spending a vigil session in the little room the author became aware of a dark figure.

Sitting in the dark, I could see enough through the knot holes in the wooden door to realise that someone was moving around on the other side although there was no sound. The door was securely locked so I could not open it to see who was there. The best I could make out from peering through the knot holes was that someone was fairly close to the door and moving around in the little entrance way to the Great Hall. I went to check by making my way back under the Solar Bar and into the Great Hall. Two of our team members were sitting on the left-hand side well away from the door. They hadn't moved but did think they had seen something moving briefly on their side of the door.

Another of the strange experiences at the Manor House concerned the big black cat who used to sleep in a favourite position in the Solar Bar by the stairs:

On one particular occasion, as we were waiting for the pub to clear at closing time, we were chatting to the landlord and finding out what, if anything, had gone on since our last visit. The landlord started to relate a tale about some carpet fitters who had been doing some work on the stairs up to the Solar Bar. These carpet fitters had become convinced that the pub was haunted by a cat because they kept hearing scratching where they were working although there was no cat to be seen. Interrupting the tale, we proceeded to say that the carpet fitters had surely only come across the pub's big black cat who was usually to be found sleeping in the Solar Bar and had probably disturbed him. At this the landlord became quite indignant and declared that there were certainly no cats in his pub because it was also a restaurant and food hygiene regulations would not allow it.

Other members of our team were asked about the big black cat who slept in the Solar Bar and curiously some had seen it regularly and others had not seen it at all. After this the cat was never seen again. The odd thing is that none of us had ever tried to touch or stroke the mysterious moggie!

The White Lion Inn Pailton

Many places we have investigated have fascinating stories associated with them but have proved to be anything but active. The White Lion Inn at Pailton near Rugby was the opposite. Very sketchy details of the reported haunting but an unexpected experience on the night.

The White Lion Inn with the old outbuilding on the left (Ian Rob, CC BY-SA 2.0)

The White Lion Inn dates back to the mid-18th century and in terms of time period is well placed to accommodate the cloaked highwayman who is reputed to haunt the area around the building and may also be the figure identified as Robert on the inside. Visitors staying in Room 6 particularly have had their night's sleep disturbed by shuffling and scraping noises. The attic rooms are the domain of Charlie, a little boy who likes to wave from the windows up there. Little more is known of these apparitions or indeed why they should be haunting the White Lion.

A small number of us had the opportunity to investigate the ancient inn after hours one night. For the most part it was very quiet, albeit atmospheric with the heavy wooden beams and décor to be expected of an 18th century inn. At the time we visited the old outbuilding to the left of the inn was just being used for storage, but this also had a reputation for being haunted. We only had access to the roof space which was by means of steep wooden steps on the outside. This had been boarded to form an upper room with exposed wooden beams over a planked walkway from the door to a small rectangular window at the furthest end of the building. The space either side of the walkway had been filled with the collected junk of many years. Walking to the far end necessitated carefully ducking under a large horizontal wooden beam stretching across the width of the building.

> In ducking under the beam my hand dropped on something that had been placed on the top. It was a 2p coin. Whilst this may seem to be an odd thing to find it must be remembered that the inn was a popular venue for ghost hunting groups. The coin had obviously been left as a trigger object. That is, something deliberately placed in the hope that it would be moved by any entity present. Having realised what it was, I carefully placed it back where it had come from.
>
> We made our way back to the door end of the roof space having decided to spend a 45-minute vigil session there. The building was in semi darkness and the first 10 minutes or so passed without incident. Then, all of a sudden, the sound of something being thrown broke the silence. With torches turned back on, a check was made to determine if anything obvious could be seen. Having earlier noted the coin on the wooden beam I immediately went to check. It was no longer there. Although the coin could not be found, this was hardly surprising given that the roof space was full of junk.

As it had been in only semi-darkness nobody in our group had moved and I know for certain I had replaced the coin where it had come from in the middle of the beam. It could not possibly have just fallen off but judging by the noise it made it was thrown with some considerable force.

Another coin was obtained and left in the same place, but the rest of the night passed without further incident, and it stayed put – perhaps waiting for the next group to find it.

Withit Witch Shop

O ne of the oldest buildings in Halesowen can be found in the relatively modern High Street pedestrianised area. The Halesowen Knitting Centre, with the superb name of Withit Witch, is an Historic England Grade II listed timber framed building with parts of it dating back to around 1452.

Grade II listed Withit Witch shop

No great wonder then that the building should be haunted. At the time we were invited to investigate some renovations were taking place upstairs. This seemed to have intensified the activity within the building, although it must be said that the haunting was never considered a problem and simply added to the hospitable atmosphere of the ancient shop. Nevertheless, it was hoped that we would be able to at least confirm some of the activity that was being experienced here. We did.

Activity here included intense cold spots even when the shop was otherwise warm, and the strong smell of tobacco smoke inside the building even though nobody smoked. The ghost had been given the name Edward and was allegedly responsible for opening and closing doors, moving objects around and even flashing the lights on and off, especially if there were any unruly children in the shop! We couldn't bring any unruly children with us unfortunately, but we did have a range of recording equipment to hopefully capture something anomalous occurring.

Our group split into pairs and the author teamed up with a representative of the shop who was staying with us for the investigation. The plan was to rotate 45-minute vigil sessions around the shop front, kitchen, and the empty rooms upstairs which were being refurbished.

It was whilst we were upstairs that the first anomalous event occurred. In just one small area of the back room, we suddenly smelt the tobacco smoke. Whilst no smoke could be seen, the smell was very strong near the centre of the room. Obviously, none of our group were smoking and we had previously checked doors and windows to make sure everything was closed. As is often the case with such potentially anomalous odours, it disappeared as quickly as it came rather than just fading away (see also the entry for Hawthorn Retirement Home).

Things really started to get interesting when we took our turn in the shop. It was around 1.00 am when we started to see little pinpoints of red light appearing randomly around the shop in the darkness. It was not our equipment and there was nothing else in the shop apart from the electronic till. Thinking it might be someone with a laser pointer outside we checked the street as well. It was deserted. The random points of lights continued for some minutes enabling more of our team to see them. Nobody could offer an explanation as to what they were. After a few minutes they ceased and did not reappear during the rest of the time we were there.

During the night we began to realise that the door at the rear of the shop, which was unlocked, was variously opened, and closed without any of the team having touched it. In view of this we placed a low-light video camera to record the area. Of course, the door did not move again. However, the camera had been moved from a larger, heavier tripod onto a lighter one to face the door so as not to be in the way. After doing this, the author and another investigator were in the shop when this happened:

> We were sitting in the shop at either end of the counter looking for the red pinpoints of light which as it happened did not reappear. All of a sudden, there was a tremendous bang from the kitchen behind us. Having no idea what this could have been we immediately went to look. The larger, heavy tripod was now lying on the floor having been pushed over. It was fortunate the camera had previously been taken off to monitor the door!

We had checked that the camera in the shop had been covering the area where the little red flashes of light were being seen. Unfortunately, it seems that the infrared lights on the camera drowned out the flashes, as although visible to our group, they were sadly not recorded when the video was played back.

Woodchester Mansion

oodchester Mansion at Nympsfield in Gloucestershire is the archetypal haunted house. It appears as an abandoned ruin deep in a secluded valley. But appearances can be deceptive. Woodchester is far from being a ruined mansion because it was never completed. Despite the fact that the house was never fully lived in, ghost stories abound, and it is one of those 'must go' places for paranormal investigators. 'Most Haunted' certainly thought so as they visited twice.

Woodchester Mansion

An original Georgian house called Spring Park was built on the site around 1750. It was in serious need of repair when William Leigh bought the 1000-acre Woodchester Estate in 1845. Leigh was a staunch Roman Catholic and a member of the controversial Oxford Movement. Spring Park was beyond economic repair according to celebrated Victorian architect, Augustus Pugin. Around 1855, work was started on a new mansion in the Victorian Gothic style designed originally by Catholic architect Charles

Hansom but later taken over by local architect Benjamin Bucknall. Progress on the new mansion was slow and with the death of William Leigh in 1873, the project was abandoned and left unfinished. Lack of money was a major factor in the house remaining uncompleted as William Leigh had spared no expense in the materials used. The house is built of local limestone and has many fine examples of carved animals, birds, and gargoyles around the building. His son and heir, also William Leigh but known as Willie, never had sufficient funds to complete his father's vision for Woodchester Mansion.

Part of the unfinished interior of Woodchester Mansion (Fiducial, CC BY-SA 3.0)

During the second world war the park was used to billet and train American troops before the D-Day landings. It was eventually purchased by Stroud District Council and looked after by Woodchester Mansion Trust. The house is restored only in as much as the original building was completed. Despite never being finished, Woodchester Mansion is Grade 1 listed and also protected due to colonies of rare Greater Horseshoe and Lesser Horseshoe Bats in two attics and the impressive bell tower.

Numerous ghosts are associated with the mansion and grounds with some being unusual to say the least if not downright bizarre. A Roman centurion has been reported near the south gate and a 'reprehensible earl' reputedly rides up and down the drive. A floating coffin has also been seen outside of the mansion and near to one of the lakes. A 'dwarf in rags', and a headless horseman are also said to frequent the grounds. Added to that, a disembodied floating head is also said to put in an appearance. Shortly before our first visit, a lady had reported seeing what she described as a glowing fog over the larger lake. It was about six feet high and three feet wide. There is also reputedly a photograph of an 'angel' taken near the same lake.

More 'conventional' ghosts here include a young girl who has been seen playing up and down the staircases. In the chapel, a short, stocky man in old fashioned working clothes stands looking up at the stonework. The presumption is that he was one of the original stonemasons. A tall, dark man has also been seen in the mansion as has a woman looking out of one of the upstairs windows as visitors arrive down the drive. The first time we visited at night there was a lady watching the drive from one of the upper windows. Not knowing the story at the time, we just assumed that she was something to do with the mansion but perhaps not?

Even seasoned investigators have not been able to spend time in the cellars because of the overwhelming feeling of something very unpleasant lurking down there. The author has spent time in the cellars and there is certainly an oppressive atmosphere and the feeling of being watched in one of the cellar rooms particularly.

The sound of 1940's style music has also been heard, although the source could never be traced. Given that the mansion and park was occupied by American servicemen prior to the D-Day landings this is perhaps not so surprising. An Irish lament has also been heard coming from the area of the kitchen, although it is unlikely that the kitchen was ever actually used as such given the lack of occupation.

Members of the Ghost Club took part in the filming of an American paranormal television programme. According to Robert Snow of the Ghost Club, at around 2.30 am in the drawing room a quiet metallic tapping was heard which got louder and louder until it reached a crescendo. Visual effects were witnessed on the wall and a control object (a two pence coin) disappeared from the kitchen area. Loud tapping sounds were heard apparently coming from upstairs but the source could not be found. In the upstairs first floor corridor a sound variously described as being like a box being dragged, a jet aircraft or an express train was heard travelling along the corridor. Amongst other sounds heard that night falling masonry was reported but no explanation could be found.

Stories are one thing, but what actually happened during our investigations certainly served to justify Woodchester Mansion's mysterious reputation. Our first investigation was organised by Paul Lee and consisted of mainly experienced ASSAP investigators. The author was accompanied by experienced investigator's Mark Hale and Gareth Goodwin. We were met by Wendy Milner who is both an ASSAP member and a voluntary guide at Woodchester Mansion. We had an initial tour around the Mansion in daylight which proved very useful. The Mansion is situated nearly a mile into the valley and is approached along a very rough and pot holed roadway. During the conducted tour, whilst we were all in the cellar area, falling stones were heard coming from the room above. No particular explanation for this was found, but stones being thrown is regularly reported at the mansion.

It was whilst we were making our way back to the mansion for the investigation that the lady in the window described above was seen. When we asked, there should not have been anyone up there as we were meeting in the drawing room to be used as our base room. Unlike most of Woodchester, this room had windows and a real fire. Most welcome on a cold night in January!

We elected to set up video recording equipment on the first floor of the building where the Ghost Club had previously heard all the unaccounted for noise in the corridor. This consisted of a high quality, low light infra-red sensitive video camera with auxiliary infra-red lighting and a VHS video recorder. This equipment was designed for long term audio and video monitoring of a location and once set up is generally left in one place. Recording periods of up to four hours at a time were possible with no operator intervention required. This setup was to prove its worth.

By 10.00 pm all equipment was set up and running and the first observation sessions started. No events of any great significance were noted during the vigil sessions that Mark, Gareth, and the author conducted. We had three sessions with these being held in the chapel, the first-floor corridor, and the cellars. All were atmospheric in their own way, and the building is a truly fascinating experience even without the paranormal activity.

During the night it was noted that the pendulum weight of the bell tower clock stored in the kitchen area was at various times swinging and the time on the face was advanced. The clock itself is a large mechanical device which was in the process of being repaired but will run if the pendulum is swung. There is no bell or other sounding device attached to the clock.

Throughout the night cows in the surrounding fields were mooing in what can best be described as a distressed manner. There was no obvious cause for this, and the staff member with us pointed out that they had not heard them making such a noise throughout the night previously. It was also intensely cold within the building though it was not freezing outside. We had not taken temperature reading devices as we knew the building to be open to the elements in parts and the wind certainly whistled through during the night.

At approximately 12.07 the single chime of a bell was heard by everyone in the drawing room which we were using as a base room. The drawing room is one of the few completed rooms in the mansion with the exception of the caretaker's living area. At the time this caused no great excitement as the sound was generally assumed to be easily explained. It was only when Wendy Milner came in and asked if everyone had heard the bell that we began to realise that it might have been unusual. It turned out that the only bell that could make such a chime was in the clock tower which was strictly out of bounds because of the rare bats living up there. There was no clock connected to the bell as this was under repair in the kitchen.

We decided to go upstairs and have a listen to the video which we hoped was still recording. On playing back the tape, at first we thought that the sound had either not been recorded or was so quiet that it was of little interest. Having decided to play the tape back right up to the point at which we stopped the recording to play it back, we were amazed to hear the clear sound of a bell perfectly recorded against the background noise of cows mooing in the fields and investigators moving around downstairs. The bell tolls once only and as far as we are aware has not been heard before or since by any of the staff or volunteers at the mansion. 🎥 1

Various theories were put forward that it could have been scaffolding or a bell in the bell tower could have been struck by something or the wind might have blown a bell causing it to toll. The possibility of it being a bell from the village church, albeit some distance away, was also discussed. On listening to the recording on a good sound system it is obvious that the sound is indeed a bell and cannot possibly be scaffolding and that the sound emanates from fairly close to the recording equipment. This assumption is based on many hours of previous recordings made on the equipment and knowledge of how it behaves in a variety of situations. At the time of the recording there was some doubt as to whether there was a bell or not still in the bell tower. Unfortunately access to the bell tower is restricted by locked grills as a colony of rare bats live up there. The only person who has access was not present on the night.

The recording of the bell was played back separately to two campanologists who had no knowledge of each other or the conditions under which the recording was made or indeed where. In both cases, they considered that the bell had been correctly struck and could not be the result of the wind blowing or any similar accidental sounding.

On the following Saturday Mark and the author were back at the mansion as guests of the Ghost Club. On this occasion we decided to set up the same recording equipment upstairs and also put a second infra-red recorder in the kitchen area to cover the clock and pendulum. We also took the opportunity to play back the bell recording to Andy, the caretaker, to see if he could throw any light on the sound. Andy said he had never heard the bell sound before and it turns out had not heard it in his part of the building on the previous weekend. He did, however, say that he had heard bangs on occasions within the building.

The first vigil session was spent upstairs near the infra-red video equipment. Almost immediately after the start of the vigil, a very loud bang was heard coming from downstairs. This was timed at 10.57 pm. At the time it was assumed that someone had slammed the front door or something similar. At 11.18 pm an exceptionally loud bang was heard again coming from downstairs. At 11.21 pm two further bangs were heard but not as loud as the first two. All of these bangs were very clearly recorded on the camera system which was situated on the first floor. 🎥 2

Investigation downstairs revealed that stone bricks had almost certainly been responsible for the bangs. The member of staff present was adamant that the building was completely safe from falling masonry and it does seem that these bricks had come down from little alcoves in the walls which would probably have taken wooden beams to hold up the floors. Half a brick had landed in the corridor outside the drawing room leaving the other half of the brick still in the alcove in the wall above. There are wooden floors downstairs which explained the loudness of the events as the bricks dropped. A possible theory for the bricks being placed in the walls is that it was done by the American film crew when the Ghost Club were here previously, but even so there appears to be no logical explanation as to why they should have fallen when they did. On this night it was noticeable that the cows were silent and the building cold but nowhere near as freezing as on the previous weekend.

One of the fallen bricks which fortunately did not hit anyone

We could find no logical explanation for either the single toll of the bell, the falling bricks or the door banging. The bell particularly appears to be a one-off event. This case is fairly unusual in that we have multiple reliable witnesses to the events, we have clear recordings, and we can be fairly certain what the events were. However, what caused the bell to toll and the bricks to drop remains a mystery. It seems unlikely that the wind could be responsible for any of these events, but in any case the wind was much stronger during the first investigation the previous week so why no bricks falling then?

A later investigation with Coventry Paranormal Investigators (CPI) proved quiet as regards loud bangs and the bell ringing was concerned. However, at around 2.00 am in the base room:

Before this investigation, I had been told by Wendy that there had recently been activity in the base room which is not normally included as a vigil location. It was about 2.00 am when a fellow investigator came and asked me if my camera in the base room was running. The tape was due to be changed but apparently one of the doors had just opened all by itself. In the event, the tape had been running and although the quality wasn't brilliant with it being an old spare recorder the door can be clearly seen slowly opening. The hinges create some resistance, and this can be heard on the recording. We weren't using the door and it had not moved previously, neither did it move again for the rest of the time we were there. 🎥 3

Unless further evidence proves otherwise, at present we have a number of potentially anomalous events witnessed and recorded on three separate occasions which in itself is unusual as far as paranormal investigations go.

🎥 1   🎥 2   🎥 3

Woody Bay North Devon

N orth Devon is steeped in myth and mystery and spending regular holidays in remote Woody Bay afforded an ideal opportunity to investigate the local ghost stories. One such story is the ghost of the old woman who walks in Woody Bay. She has been seen on more than one occasion but does an old holiday snap prove her existence?

Woody Bay North Devon

Woody Bay lies down the coast from picturesque Lynton and Lynmouth. A narrow coast road leads through the dramatic Valley of the Rocks but beware, as a horse-drawn coach and at least one car have plunged several hundred feet from the narrow cliff road to destruction on the rugged rocks below. The A39 is a much newer, and safer, alternative. A steeply winding road leads down from the National Trust car park and ends at what were probably old limeworker's cottages (now holiday lets). The remains of the limestone kilns are not far away. A footpath then carries on to the rocky beach and magnificent hanging waterfall beneath the deeply wooded cliffs.

Another narrower footpath can be found winding its way up to the road above. This is Sir Robert's Path, leading up over Inkerman Bridge, and named after Sir Robert Chichester who lived at the time of King James I. Old family papers discovered in the 19th century refer to the somewhat infamous Sir Robert. 'The old mansion of Crosscomb in the parish of Martinhoe, is said to have once been the seat of Sir Robert Chichester, of whose crimes and supernatural appearances after death, many traditions are still preserved among the older peasants'. His ghost is said to haunt the base of the cliffs where in one version of the story he is cursed to weave a rope out of sand in order to haul his carriage up the path named after him. An impossible task of course, but there are far worse places than Woody Bay to spend eternity!

The path is also locally known as 'the ghost path' but nothing to do with Sir Robert it seems. Two young couples staying at Martinhoe Manor in the 1980s had spent a pleasant evening at the Woody Bay Hotel on the coast road above and were returning in the dark down Sir Robert's Path. Having just passed Inkerman Bridge the two young ladies were walking ahead when they were both tapped on the back. Assuming it was their partners trying to scare them, they ignored it the first time. The second time it happened they both turned around but instead of their partners they were faced with what they described as a green, glowing hooded figure. The girls screamed and ran. By the time the men caught up there was no sign of what they described as a 'ghostly green monk'. Naturally, they were very shaken up by the experience which they described in detail at the time to George, the manager of Martinhoe Manor. Now of course they could have simply made the whole thing up for devilment, except that it caused one of the young ladies to have an asthma attack which she had not suffered from for years. She and her partner promptly left Woody Bay the very next day.

During one of many family holidays staying at Martinhoe Manor, we had made our way down to the rocky beach for the afternoon. The tide comes in very quickly here and unwary visitors have been dangerously cut off as there is only one path back up. On this particular afternoon it was very quiet with only a handful of people on the beach. We couldn't help but notice a young couple with a wicker picnic hamper. We thought they were celebrating something, perhaps an engagement, as the young man was dressed in what appeared to be a vintage striped blazer with a straw boater and the young lady was wearing a similar period costume. They looked like extras from Downton Abbey. We tried not to stare of course but noticed that they settled themselves behind some rocks a bit further down the beach from us and opened what looked like a bottle of Champagne. As the afternoon wore on, the tide started to come in and along with the few other people down there we made our way back up to the path. The strange thing was that there was no sign of the young couple. They hadn't already left as we would have seen them, and they definitely did not come back up from the beach with everyone else. Woody Bay can be a very strange place at times.

A figure in a shawl can be seen crossing the path to the cottage

The photograph of the path to the limeworker's cottages was taken in the mid-1980s before the prevalence of digital cameras. Right of centre, a form can be made out which bears a striking resemblance to an old woman in a long dress holding a shawl around her shoulders. She appears to be crossing the path from the little walled garden on the right. The position of the figure is clearly shown in the drawing.

The position of the figure in the photograph

The figure could be put down to prevailing lighting conditions or the shadows of bushes. However, according to Harriet Bridle's book, *Woody Bay*, 'individually and on two separate occasions' visitors to Martinhoe Manor have witnessed the apparition of an old lady dressed in grey, passing through the wall below the cottage at exactly the same spot as the figure in the photograph. One of the witnesses, a retired nurse not prone to flights of fancy, enquired whether there had been a door or gate in the wall there at one time. There may well have been as the present building is a refurbished combination of two 18th century limeworker's cottages which had fallen derelict by the 1930s, so it seems very likely that there have been major alterations to the site over the years.

How can we be sure that it is not a real person on the path? The photograph was taken by the author on the last day of a week's holiday in late October. There was nobody else on the path that afternoon and no sign of anything unusual in the viewfinder. It was not until the film was developed that the figure became apparent. Is she a shade or just a shadow? If indeed a shade, we shall probably never know who the old lady is or why she still walks in Woody Bay.

Would you believe it?

Things are not always quite what they seem. This is as true for paranormal investigators as is it for those who believe they have been witness to paranormal events. Here is a selection of some particularly memorable examples gathered over many years.

Medieval Knight

A long passage ran through the Sharrington Range at Dudley Castle (see main entry) to a small display area, and then out through what was once a shop. The displays reflected very much the medieval life of the castle and knights in armour.

Sharrington Range with entry to the Visitor Centre on the left

Knowing that footsteps had been reported in this area the author with fellow investigator Gareth, set up a low light level video camera in the darkness and waited.

After about 30 minutes or so we started to hear faint sounds in the distance. These sounds got louder and louder and they were clearly heavy footsteps. Not only that but the footsteps were accompanied by what sounded very much like armour clanking. A quick check of the camera and the infrared lights proved that it was recording and so we waited.

The noise got louder and louder. The corridor we were in was quite long and had a right-angled bend further down. By now it was obvious that we were in the same corridor as whatever was coming towards us. We waited for it to appear around the bend in the corridor and then a figure emerged out of the darkness. It was dressed in what appeared to be medieval garb with knee length boots and chains making all the noise. We stood our ground and the figure approached. "Hello guys, how's it going?", is not quite what one would expect from the apparition of a medieval knight and, of course, it was nothing of the sort.

Jamie, who used to lead the Dudley castle ghost walks in full costume, had seen his group safely off site but had decided to join us for a night of paranormal investigating. He was just passing through to get changed.

Expect the Unexpected

Before one of our many investigations at Dudley Castle we had been told about an apparition seen from within the shop in the Sherrington Range. A shadowy figure of a lady had been seen and one of the shop assistants said she had seen the lower half of a figure in Victorian style dress whilst the doors from the shop to the visitor centre had been open. A wooden exit door from the medieval display led directly into the shop. Beneath this door there was a wide gap between the bottom and the stone floor.

In the gap, shop assistants had also reported seeing what they described as a 'long swishing skirt' as might have been worn by a lady in period dress. In view of this, we set-up a low light level video camera trained on the door. With the lights on in the display corridor behind and off in the shop, anything moving around would be seen and recorded. This what happened:

The author was sat immediately behind the camera looking at the door. After a while sitting in the darkness, something started to move. A dark shifting shape could be seen clearly silhouetted in the gap between the bottom of the door and the stone floor. Never mind ghosts, my thoughts turned to the venomous bird eating spiders kept not too far away in the Discovery Centre and whether one of them had escaped. If it had, it was big. I'm ashamed to admit panic set in and I shouted to my colleague Gareth to turn the lights on quick! Very gingerly we approached the door to see what was there. It was

Gareth who found him. Showing far more fortitude than I could muster he put his hand into a small gap in the wall and gently lifted out a natterjack toad. He had obviously found his way in and had been parading up and down behind the door. Needless to say, he was returned safely to the grounds. In over 25 years of investigating, it is the one and only time I have ever yelled to have the lights turned back on during a vigil!

Haunted Hare

Haunted dolls seem to have taken on a life of their own so to speak in recent years. This case did not involve a doll, but a novelty cuddly toy—a haunted hare in fact. It had all started when the witness and some friends used a Ouija board during a party at her house.

'Ouija Board' painting by Norman Rockwell

Ouija Boards, as with dowsing and other such techniques, operate because of something called the ideomotor response. These are subconscious muscle movements. In fact, with a pendulum it is possible to simply think clockwise or anti-clockwise and the weight or 'bob' will oblige. Now, opinions vary greatly on Ouija boards from a purely psychological phenomena at one end of the scale to an open invitation to let demons into your home at the other. Much of course depends on personal belief but it is the author's opinion that they can be harmful at a psychological level to susceptible people, and in any case are not a valid and reliable tool for paranormal investigations. In any event, the author has never seen a Ouija board planchette moving of its own accord without one or more participants having their fingers placed on it. And if it did, that really would be something interesting.

But back to the case. The author had a call from a friend, we will call her Eileen, who was in something of a panic. She was convinced that a novelty cuddly toy had become possessed and wanted me to come and remove it for her as she didn't even want to touch it.

On arriving at Eileen's Edwardian terraced house, I got the full story. Apparently, she had invited some friends over for a party and someone had brought a Ouija board with them. Thinking it would be fun to try and contact the 'spirits', they had turned the lights down in the living room and immediately started using the board. According to Eileen, nothing was done to try and prevent any negative or unwelcome energies from coming through. "It was mostly nonsense at first until suddenly the glass seemed to take on a life of its own. It raced around the board and spelt out the name Jack".

Jack went on to spell out how he had once lived in the house before being called up to fight in the First World War where he met his untimely end. However, the session had to be brought to an abrupt finish when the entity suddenly turned nasty, spelling out swear words and making threats. Eileen was naturally extremely upset by all of this, especially as she lived alone and wished they had never messed with the Ouija board in the first place.

In need of a stiff drink and a change of scene after the amateur séance they had all gone into the front room. Eileen had recently bought a novelty cuddly toy, a long-eared hare, for her nieces to play with when they visited. It was battery powered and had its own remote control. When triggered, it would jig around on the spot and speak a selection of pre-programmed phrases.

Eileen explained what happened next, "As we were all sitting around in the front room with the lights dimmed ready to play a video game the hare suddenly burst into life, saying "Will you be my friend?" and jigging on its shelf even though nobody had touched the remote control. At this point they were all thoroughly freaked out by these experiences and couldn't get out of the front room fast enough. Eileen was absolutely convinced that the hare was now possessed by the nasty spirit of Jack. It hadn't helped that she had recently watched a television programme on haunted dolls and by now Eileen was too terrified to even touch the hare let alone throw it away.

> The obvious thing to do was recreate the sequence of events as closely as possible following the Ouija board séance. We went into the front room to take a look and I proceeded to ask exactly what she and her friends had been doing. It turned out they were having a drink and playing a video game of 'Who Wants to be a Millionaire?'. Well, after no more than two or three presses of the video game's remote control the 'possessed' hare duly burst into life and asked if I wanted to be his friend!

No more possessed hare but one very much relieved Eileen when she realised it had only been the quiz game's remote control interfering with the cuddly toy after all.

After-Life Sentence

Oxford Gaol has now been converted into a swish boutique hotel, although part of it is now the Oxford Castle and Prison visitor experience.

Oxford Prison (Gordon Griffiths, CC BY-SA 2.0)

Previous to the renovation work members of ASSAP had a unique opportunity to investigate the original prison.

Originally Oxford Castle, Empress Matilda escaped from her cousin Stephen in the 12th century during the civil war known as the 'Anarchy'. Her ghost, dressed in a white cloak, reputedly wanders the older part of the building. An ill-mannered monk smelling of alcohol also frequents what is left of the former castle and it is said can be heard swearing and cursing. Mary Blandy, who allegedly poisoned her father with arsenic and was hung for the crime refuses to leave the place of her execution. Doors open and close on their own for no reason and can sometimes be heard slamming shut. Last but not least, a dark, shadowy figure had been seen wandering the wings of the later prison.

We divided up into small teams and areas were allocated by the vigil coordinator. Our team was in one wing of cells connected by long corridor to another wing of similar cells. The author was positioned at one end of this corridor. Every few yards there was a small alcove on either side leading to a cell door.

As I sat there staring into the semi darkness, I began to fancy I could see someone at the other end of the corridor. I quietly moved a few yards in and stepped into the first alcove to get a closer look. Sure enough, for a few seconds there was a black figure standing at the other end. Was this the ghost who wanders the wings? I moved slowly and quietly further into the corridor to try and get a better view. There was no doubt the figure was still there, and we were getting closer. With only a few yards to go I stepped out and stood in the corridor to confront whatever it was. As I did so, the dark figure also stopped and appeared to be looking at me. We both walked slowly forward. A fellow investigator from another group had been doing exactly the same as me. He thought I was the wandering ghost!

Phantom Bar Staff

At the Red Lion Inn in Avebury (see main entry), activity seemed to be focused mainly in the dining room at the rear of the pub, known for poltergeist type occurances. During one of our investigations, the author and fellow investigator, Mark, were sitting in a small bar area.

The Red Lion Avebury (Beltanemoon, CC BY-SA 4.0)

It was now 3.00 am, and all of a sudden the electronic till on the bar sprang to life and lit up as though someone was using it although there was nobody anywhere near. We moved over to it and the screen was displaying what appeared to be customer orders at high speed. As we were watching, somewhat amazed, the till felt silent again and the lights went out.

It might not sound much in the cold light of day, but it certainly came as a surprise at 3.00 am in a quiet, dark pub. The following morning, we related the whole event to the Duty Manager. We thought his response might be disbelief, but no. In fact, he laughed. "Oh yes", he said, "it does that at 3.00 am every morning". Apparently, the computer till was timed to transmit the day's takings down the phone line to a central computer. To do this it had to first turn itself on. He might have told us the night before. Feeling foolish does not quite describe it!

The Picture Poltergeist

Having been called in to investigate a possible poltergeist in Kidderminster, George Gregg and the author arranged to interview the couple concerned. The young man was an avid watcher of 'reality' paranormal programmes on television and so when their photographs started flying off the walls in the living room it had to be a poltergeist. Never mind that this was causing his partner to be afraid in her own home. Also, their cat would sit and stare at the wall in the living room for long periods of time for no apparent reason.

Having noted all of this down, we took a look at the remaining photographs. It turned out that the flat was rented, and they did not want to risk any damage by drilling into the walls. They had used Blu Tack instead. Blue Tack is useful as a temporary fix for many things but not for permanently attaching pictures to walls. Eventually, the weight causes the inevitable to happen. Gravity takes over and the pictures fall to the floor. Added to that, depending on how they fall, the pictures may glide for some way before reaching the floor the giving the impression that they have been thrown. To say the young lady was relieved is an understatement. No poltergeist then. And the staring cat? We explained it is simply in the nature of cats. They do that kind of thing for a variety of mundane reasons.

Something in the Cellar

The Old Mill in Upper Gornal is a lovely old Victorian public house dating back to 1852. It was the site of one of our investigations after reports of poltergeist activity. Things would get moved around and loud inexplicable bangs were being heard.

The Old Mill in Upper Gornal

Our investigation started after the pub had closed for the night. Odd bumps and bangs could indeed be heard but this may just have been the building settling. Shortly after midnight, we started experiencing sudden localised temperature drops. One of our team saw a shadow pass over a picture in the lounge. Very shortly after, the author and a colleague clearly saw a shadow moving behind the bar. Another member of our team saw what she described as a 'frightening form' in the lounge near to the cellar door. Then this happened:

> The author was sitting not far from the door to the cellar, which we had access to. All of a sudden, the silence was shattered by a loud banging sound coming from the cellar. Typical poltergeist activity. We had deliberately kept the cellar free of investigators to hopefully encourage something to happen and here it was. We all made a dash for the cellar door. Being closest, I made it first and threw myself down the narrow, winding steps to catch whatever it was. Now some people might think the sensible idea would be to run in the opposite direction, but this was, after all, what we were here for. I had fully expected the noise to stop before reaching the bottom of the steps, but no. The cause of all the commotion was there, right in front of me. The automatic ice machine was busy firing ice cubes into a metal bucket!

Lady Eleanor's Room

One of our investigations took us to Whittington Castle in Shropshire. This 12th century Marcher Castle once guarded the border with Wales. It has legendary associations with the Holy Grail and Robin Hood through the Fitzwarine family.

A number of ghosts are said to haunt Whittington Castle and nowadays it is popular with commercial ghost hunts. A hooded figure is reputedly seen beneath the gateway and may have connections with the Robin Hood legend. A more unusual ghost is that of a blacksmith complete with leather apron. The faces of children have also been seen peering out of one of the upstairs windows.

We found the castle and its surroundings to be very atmospheric. Parts of the castle had been restored including Lady Eleanor's Room where weddings are now conducted. With the doors closed and in the early hours of the morning, this room was pitch black inside. There were a few chairs around the walls and a table with an old Bible on it at the front of the room. One of our team placed a EMF metre on this, which had a small red LED light to show it was switched on.

Whittington Castle (Peter Craine, CC BY-SA 2.0)

As we sat there in the darkness, one by one the members of our team started saying the book was moving. Lady Eleanor herself perhaps? More precisely, the little red LED on top of the book was moving, so the book must have been moving as well, although of course it could not be seen in the dark. We watched for a few minutes and sure enough the light was dancing around. At times it would seem to rise to the ceiling or float from side to side. If a light was shone on it though, the book and the LED would be back where they started.

So, what was going on? Nothing to do with anything paranormal or Lady Eleanor unfortunately. It is a known phenomenon called the Autokinetic Effect. In a darkened room it is impossible to stare at a point of light without it appearing to dance around. It is caused by slight eye movements and our brains having no real points of reference to create a steady image.

In fact, the author has seen this very same effect used on commercial ghost hunts and with a little bit of theatre provided by the organisers can have the unwary really believing they are witnessing something paranormal.

Orbs

During our initial investigation at Katie's Café (see main entry) we had our very first experience of the phenomena known as orbs. If paranormal television programmes at the time were to be believed we were looking at early manifestations of spirit. And why not, we were after all in an allegedly haunted building.

Two different types of 'orb' at Drakelow Tunnels

We had with us our first professional low-light digital video camera. This had infrared lights for night vision and was attached to a portable video recorder. As soon as it was set up and recording the main area of interest at the top of the stairs, we began to see moving 'orbs' on the monitor. These appeared as white circles moving randomly in front of the lens.

Initial excitement though soon gave way to a more rational investigation of the phenomena in front of us. It soon became apparent that the white circles were being caused by dust particles in the air. These out of focus particles close to the lens create what is called a circle of confusion. Added to this, illumination from camera lights or a flash can cause an effect known as backscatter where light is reflected back from near objects such as dust and can often be seen as a brightly illuminated circle or 'orb'. Digital camera image noise, a known issue, can also contribute to the structure often seen in orbs.

Since the prevalence of digital cameras orbs have become commonplace. The reason is to do with lens aperture and focal length. Digital cameras often have a small aperture which means the depth of field (or focus) is quite close to the lens. All sorts of stray particles including dust and pollen can create orbs as can passing insects. The latter can appear to be quite spectacular, especially when caught on an infrared security camera.

Even years later, opinions on orbs are very much divided and they are a regular topic of lively debate on paranormal social media sites. Many people believe orbs to be manifestations of spirit whilst others put them down to being just dust and insects. Some paranormal investigators take a middle ground and maintain that there are indeed some orbs that cannot be explained rationally.

It is the author's belief that visible light anomalies certainly do exist and there are a number of examples in this book. However, where visual effects such as orbs can only be seen on camera, they are much more likely to be artefacts created by airborne particles too small to be seen or insects which are often attracted to infrared lights.

Lady in Waiting

If you have not already done so, have a look at the pictures of Chillingham Castle in Northumberland and decide in your own mind what it is you are looking at in the window. An original, full colour version can also be viewed here. 🎥 1

Chillingham Castle

Enlarged view of right hand tower window

Is that really a lady standing watching from the window?

Even the very name, Chillingham, hints towards its dark past with creepy dungeons, terrifying torture chamber and a history of misery and death. No surprise then that the castle has an enviable reputation for being haunted and has featured regularly on television programmes such as Fox Family Channel's Scariest Places on Earth. One of the many ghosts reported here is the famous 'Radiant Boy' who haunts one of the bedrooms. He was known to scream in pain or terror on the stroke of midnight and a boy dressed in blue would appear through a halo of light. The bones of a child and fragments of blue cloth were discovered where the apparition would appear. Following a Christian burial, the 'Radiant Boy' seemed to be at peace except blue flashes of light are still seen in the night by people staying in the same bedroom.

The most interesting ghost story though is that of Lady Mary Berkeley who died in 1719. She was the ill-fated wife of Lord Grey of Wark and Chillingham. He preferred the affections of her younger sister, Henrietta, after Mary had given birth to a daughter. The whole affair caused an awful scandal in 18th century aristocratic society. Poor Lady Mary was left to wander the lonely castle with her baby, yearning for the return of her unfaithful husband. He never did return, and her unquiet spirit is said to be still residing in the castle, forlornly waiting for her long-lost love to come home.

A surprise birthday present one year was a ghost hunt night-time tour of Chillingham Castle. The group was limited to around 25 people, and we were some of the first to arrive. Having a little bit of spare time gave opportunity to get some photographs before the main event officially started. Nothing untoward was noticed when taking pictures of the castle. The tour was led by a very knowledgeable guide and is to be recommended to anyone visiting Northumberland with an interest in ghosts and hauntings.

It was only after we had returned home that a potential anomaly on one of the pictures was noticed. The camera was a high-resolution Nikon SLR and enabled zooming in without too much loss of detail. The apparent criss-cross pattern is caused by the window concerned being leaded. Having noticed the apparent figure staring out of the window, I contacted the castle to ask if anyone was likely to have been in the room concerned. It turned out that there was nobody in that particular part of the castle before the tour and nothing in the room that could explain the image. To this day, it has to remain unexplained.

So what is it? There is a known phenomenon called pareidolia where basically our brains try to make sense of random patterns and produce a meaningful image. This explains why we can often seem to see faces in clouds and wallpaper for example. Is this then a prime example of pareidolia or is it the ghost of Lady Mary looking out of the window for her errant husband?

And Finally ...

We have often joked over the years that a really useful poltergeist would be one that did the housework. For one witness who contacted us this did actually seem to be the case.

The witness was a young, hardworking single mother who lived in a ground floor flat with her toddler daughter. Always in a rush to get to nursery and work in the mornings, breakfast cereal spilt by the daughter would often be simply left on the kitchen floor until they got home again. By this time, the food would invariably be gone and the kitchen floor clean. Thanks mainly to the proliferation of paranormal television programmes, the answer was obvious. She had a poltergeist in the flat.

Thinking that this particular poltergeist might have short grey fur and a very long tail we very tactfully, or so we thought, suggested that a Pest Control Officer might be a more logical place to start than a paranormal investigation team.

We never heard from her again.

🎥 1

Bibliography

Alexander, M., *Haunted Inns* (Muller, 1973).

Arnall, C., *Mysterious Occurrences* (Davies, 2009).

Bell, D., *Ghosts and Legends of Staffordshire* (Countryside, 1994).

Bradford, A., *Haunted Pubs and Hotels of Worcestershire* (Hunt End), 1998).

Bradford, A., *The Haunted Midlands* (Brewin Books 2006).

Glews, P., *Dudley Through Time* (Amberley Publishing, 2010.

Green, A., *Haunted Inns and Taverns* (Shire, 1995).

Hallam, J., *The Haunted Inns of England* (Wolfe, 1972).

Hawthorne, B., *Black Country and Birmingham Ghost Stories* (Bradwell, (2013).

Homer, A. and Taylor, D., *Beer and Spirits* (Amberley Publishing, 2010).

Homer, A., A *Black Country Miscellany* (Tin Typewriter, 2016).

Homer, A., *Black Country Ghosts and Hauntings* (Tin Typewriter, 2017).

Homer, A., *Haunted Hostelries of Shropshire* (Amberley Publishing, 2012).

Lewis, M., *Conclusions of a Parapsychologist* (BalboaPress, 2013.

Perrins, A., *Ghosts and Folklore around Barr Beacon* (Perrins, 2001).

Playfair, G. L., *The Haunted Pub Guide* (Harrap, 1985).

Poulton-Smith., A., *Black Country Ghosts* (The History Press, 2010).

Solomon, P., *Haunted Black Country* (The History Press, 2010).

List of videos

Alton Towers Clip 1 https://youtu.be/7-gprIJngCE

Black Country Living Museum Clip 1 https://youtu.be/cwfL3Gqzz8A

Bonded Warehouse Clip 1 https://youtu.be/hOhIxAf7JP0

Chillingham Castle Clip 1 https://youtu.be/r1n-G6x3R_4

Drakelow Tunnels Clip 1 https://youtu.be/xdXe2NbURwM

Gresley Old Hall Clip 1 https://youtu.be/DXnHNi_F5T4

Guy's Cliffe House Clip 1 https://youtu.be/stDqgk6WutI

Mason's Ironstone Pottery Cip 1 https://youtu.be/PvQimfvB-oY

Spar Shop Much Wenlock Clip 1 https://youtu.be/hNzG0QifDLY

Spar Shop Much Wenlock Clip 2 https://youtu.be/PpDQY6omsSI

Starving Rascal Amblecote Clip 1 https://youtu.be/ZVlkL7RZGfA

The Belgrave Triangle Clip 1 https://youtu.be/mmt7a3Kzr7A

Woodchester Mansion Clip 1 https://youtu.be/RuoJtwJP_qk

Woodchester Mansion Clip 2 https://youtu.be/B-66JwQDDU0

Woodchester Mansion Clip 3 https://youtu.be/667kUtCpA6U

About the author

Andrew Homer has written several books on ghosts, hauntings and history. He has an MA in West Midlands History awarded by the University of Birmingham and is also a former Secretary of the Black Country Society.

Andrew has spent over 25 years investigating paranormal phenomena with a number of serious, scientific based groups. For most of this time he was an Accredited Investigator, and later member of the National Register of Professional Investigators maintained by the Association for the Scientific Study of Anomalous Phenomena (ASSAP). During this time Andrew was awarded the Michael Bentine Shield by ASSAP for work on the remarkable Hawthorn Retirement Home case included here.

Andrew has presented lectures on both hauntings and history to numerous organisations and has appeared on local and national television. He enjoys collecting ghost stories, particularly those which have historical connections. Andrew also enjoys a pint of real ale preferably served in a traditional Black Country public house.

Andrew can be contacted through his website at:

www.andrewhomer.co.uk

By the same author

Black Country Ghosts and Hauntings – Tin Typewriter Publishing

Haunted Hostelries of Shropshire – Amberley Publishing

Beer and Spirits – Amberley Publishing

A Question of the Black Country – Tin Typewriter Publishing

Secret Black Country – Amberley Publishing

A–Z of the Black Country – Amberley Publishing

A–Z of Birmingham – Amberley Publishing

Historic England: The Black Country – Amberley Publishing

Historic England: Birmingham – Amberley Publishing

A Black Country Miscellany – Tin Typewriter Publishing

THE BLACK COUNTRY SOCIETY

The Black Country Society was founded in 1967 as a reaction to the trends of the late 1950s and early 1960s. This was a time when the reorganisation of local government was seen as a threat to the identity of individual communities and when, in the name of progress and modernisation, the industrial heritage of the Black Country was in danger of being swept away.

The general aims of the Society are to stimulate interest in the past, present and future of the Black Country and wherever possible, to encourage and facilitate the preservation of Black Country heritage.

The Society, which now has a large membership worldwide, organises an annual programme of social activities including 'Talks' at local venues, and guided 'Walks' on evenings during the Summer months, around the Black Country and its green borderland.

The Society sponsors and publishes material by Black Country writers and researchers. It has an extensive catalogue of books on subjects ranging from humour and cooking, to industrial history and sport. Further information on all activities are to be found on the website, facebook page and in the Society's quarterly, full colour, 96 page magazine 'The Blackcountryman'.

www.blackcountrysociety.com